BEHIND
BARBED
WIRE

by Vinnie Ruffo

PACIFIC PRESS PUBLISHING ASSOCIATION

Mountain View, California   Omaha, Nebraska

Dedicated to Paul, my husband, whose patience and quiet inspiration helped me write this book.

INTRODUCTION

John and Olga Oss sailed for the Orient in 1919. Arriving in China, they attended language school for six months, and eventually became fluent in the difficult Chinese language.

First the mission board called them to serve in Manchuria, where for the next four and one half years John had charge of the Publishing Department and Olga worked with women colporteurs, training them for service. Their travels took them to the borders of Siberia. Later, John was transferred to Shanghai, where he headed the publishing work in the heavily populated East China Union Mission. In time, he was asked to lead the forces of literature evangelism in all of China. He became editor in chief of the *Signs of the Times,* serving until World War II, when China was involved in all-out war.

Olga labored diligently to raise funds for the building of a clinic for the poor in the city of Shanghai. Her special ability in reaching the hearts and purse strings of the rich enabled the church to carry out plans for a clinic. With Marie Miller, Olga brought in thousands of dollars. One Manchurian military leader alone gave $400,000. When the clinic was finished, a dream had become reality. Here the destitute could receive medical treatment for only 20 coppers (three cents). Here, until invaders seized the hospital, countless thousands were served.

When the war started in December, 1941, mission workers were among the first to be apprehended. They became prisoners-at-large until the Japanese interned them in a prison camp known as the Chapei Civilian Assembly Center, outside Shanghai. *Behind Barbed Wire* is the story of the internment of Pastor and Mrs. Oss in that prison camp for thirty-one months. It is also an outstanding story of God's continual watchcare and providence.

THE PUBLISHERS

CONTENTS

Whose Shall These Riches Be? 1

Shanghai, queen city of the Orient, trembled with fear. Junks, sampan dwellings creaking with families, and paddlewheel boats jammed the muddy waters of the Whangpoo River. Everywhere the hustle and bustle of carts and people added excitement. Along Nanking Road, the Times Square area of Shanghai, a sweaty, ragged, half-starved coolie pulled a heavy ricksha. Faster and faster his bony feet slapped the pavement.

"Hurry, hurry, fool," yelled his rotund, silk-clad passenger. Ringing his bell with fury, the coolie cleared a zigzag path through the traffic, dodging pedestrians, carts, and other rickshas.

Directly behind this ricksha, another followed, carrying a tiny woman. The second coolie tried desperately to keep pace. His Chinese passenger, her face rutted by age, wore a look of fear and urgency. The coolies raced past gambling halls and noisy marts. It seemed that Shanghai's millions, crowding the city everywhere, moved with frenzied haste and excitement and a kind of paralyzing fear. Many sought escape in dingy opium dens.

Famine, floods, futility—the regal city had experienced and survived them all. Now she waited with dread anticipation. Another enemy lurked on her muddy doorstep. It seemed only a matter of days until all-out war with Japan would erupt—maybe only hours, even minutes. For months hostile gunboats had lined the waters of the Whangpoo River, poised and ready to blast.

The first coolie panted to a halt before the high walls of the Seventh-day Adventist mission compound on Ningkuo Road. The second pulled up only a few paces behind him. The passenger of obvious means leaped out and ran to help the elderly woman.

Tossing a coin into the sweating palm of each coolie, he hurried to the gate of the compound.

Inside, Olga Oss, Adventist missionary from America, sat alone in her home. John, her husband, editor in chief of *Signs of the Times* in Hong Kong and Shanghai, was often gone. This time he had been away for several days and was now expected back any minute.

Glancing nervously at her watch, she wondered why he hadn't returned. What was keeping him? Rumors of impending hostilities worried her. She spoke aloud, "Please, John, hurry back."

A soft knock on the door startled her.

John wouldn't knock. Who could this be?

In a moment Su Deh, the Chinese servant girl, entered. "People to see you," she announced, bowing. "Strangers."

A flutter of excitement passed through Olga. Strangers? On a day when the air was heavy with premonition. Who could they be? "All right, Su Deh; let them in."

Su Deh ushered the visitors into the room. Olga found herself facing the prune-wrinkled woman of the ricksha and the well-dressed man who preceded her. He stepped forward and bowed. "I am Low Sing, and this is my mother. We have been told that you and your husband are missionaries." The same urgency of the day was in his voice. "Soon—very soon—there will be war. It is not safe for us—our family—to remain in Shanghai. We will go south, to Foochow. And we have come to ask a favor of you."

Olga sensed instantly that this man was facing a serious problem. But why had he come to her? What could she do? She invited them to be seated and had Su Deh bring in a pot of flower tea, for thus it is done in China. No caller is even allowed to state his business without first being served refreshments. The servant poured the tea, bowed graciously, and left. This gesture was the signal for brief "polite conversation" to begin. But Low Sing had no time for customary proprieties.

"May I use your dining-room table?" he asked.

"Of course," Olga answered politely. But what was he up to?

Low Sing reached into his pocket and pulled out a small chamois pouch, secured with a drawstring. Olga watched intently while he turned the pouch upside down and poured the contents on the table.

Olga gasped. What a sight! She couldn't believe what she saw. Strewn on the table, dazzling with matchless brilliancy, were diamonds, hundreds of them. Large and small. Turning to face Low Sing, she found herself at a loss for words. Whatever could this mean—all this fabulous wealth poured out for her to see?

Low Sing stepped to the table and separated the gems into two piles—large and small. "Go ahead," he invited. "Touch them. Do not be afraid."

Awestruck, Olga could only reply, "No, no, I'm not used to handling precious stones. These must be worth thousands of dollars." She moved a few paces from the table.

Low Sing smiled. "Yes, many, many thousands." Slowly, then, he dropped each precious stone back into the pouch and tucked the treasure into his pocket.

The wrinkled mother waved a tiny hand. "Wait, I too have something to show you." Reaching into a pocket inside her brocaded dress, she pulled out another pouch. Her hands trembled as she emptied its contents on the table. Again Olga gasped. Before her lay a bracelet made of pure jade, resplendent with scores of diamonds.

Olga could not help exclaiming, "Why, this is the most beautiful bracelet I have ever seen!" She fingered the exquisite object. "But, but why have you brought these things here?"

Again urgency showed in Low Sing's voice. "We must leave the city, and leave quickly. We have no time to spare. If the Japanese attack before we get away, they will seize all our treasure. We have chosen to come to you because our friends told us that you were missionaries and you would help us. We want you to hide the diamonds for us."

Olga dropped into a chair. So this was it. She wished John were present. Why did things like this happen to her when he was away? Maybe this was some kind of crazy scheme. It was unthinkable that she could become involved with all these diamonds.

Speaking firmly but kindly, she said, "I really don't see why we should become a party to your plans."

Impatience that could not be hidden creased Low Sing's face. "Don't you see? Soon—very soon—the Japanese will invade the city and will seize all our possessions. You *must* hide them for us."

Olga was silent. Questions rose to her lips.

Seeing her hesitancy, Low Sing pleaded, "Mrs. Oss, we do not believe the Japanese will bother white missionaries. They would never think to look for diamonds here in your home."

Olga wished she could feel as secure about their future as he did.

"You are our only hope," Low Sing pressed. "You *must* preserve our wealth for us." Pacing the floor, he groped for words to gain her consent. "You have a brick house. All we have to do is remove a few bricks, hide the diamonds, and no one will ever suspect."

The old woman took a few steps and placed a hand on Olga's arm. "You alone can hide our wealth for us."

Olga felt her head spinning. Surely she wanted to help these people. It would be a tragedy if they were to lose their wealth. But—

And then the tempter whispered a sly suggestion, "Olga, just think, if they never came back, all this treasure would be yours— yours and John's. You would be rich—fabulously rich. And," he added piously, "you could help all the starving people with this treasure. And if Low Sing does come back, he would reward you handsomely. Does not God provide for His own?"

Olga was tempted. Then somehow she snapped herself out of the deceiver's clutch. "Get thee behind me, Satan," she commanded. Not that she didn't want to help Low Sing and his mother. But to place the mission in a compromising position and thus give occasion to muckrakers to slander missionaries as rich exploiters of the unfortunate—that she could not risk doing. The mission compound would doubtless be the first place invaders would search. And if they discovered diamonds, what would they say? She visualized their names, publicized with sarcasm, "American missionaries found with fabulous wealth hidden in house."

Seeking to dissuade Low Sing from his purpose, she said, "You forget that the Japanese have detectors all over and could discover the diamonds."

"But they wouldn't find them behind the bricks," he insisted.

Low Sing's desperation tormented Olga. What would John do? What would he say? But being unable to consult him, she rechecked her own reasoning, weighing the pros and cons. If the Japanese found the treasure in this house, what reproach this would bring upon the church, upon Christianity in general. This maneuver could cast a shadow that would never fade. The enemy would love this. On the other hand—could not this be providential? Was God providing the money so desperately needed for their missionary work?

At this point Su Deh entered the room prepared to pour the second round of tea. Glancing at the standing guests and untouched teacups, she decided instead to make a quick exit.

"Mrs. Oss, *please* will you hide our diamonds?" Low Sing persisted.

Olga faced her visitors, her answer on her lips.

Speaking with determination she said, "No, no, I cannot bring reproach upon the church. Don't you see what would happen if the Japanese *did* find the diamonds here in this house?"

Making one last desperate plea, Low Sing cried, "Mrs. Oss, I do not believe they could ever find them behind the bricks unless they tore down the whole house."

"No, no, I am truly sorry. But I cannot help you. I cannot do this thing." Her answer came from a heavy heart.

Low Sing bowed politely, "We are sorry, very, very sorry, too." A moment later, the rich man, his mother, and all their fabulous jewels were gone.

As Olga watched them walk slowly out of the gate, she reflected on another aspect of the drama she had just witnessed: Why, oh why could not those whom God had made stewards of such wealth give to help the plight of humanity before some tragic turn of events compelled them to part with their treasures? Why did people cling to their possessions as if they could enjoy them forever?

Alone again, Olga was plagued by doubt. Had she made the right decision? Did God want *them* instead of the Japanese to have the treasure?

Suddenly she found a thousand thoughts hurrying through her harrassed mind. Events of their twenty-two years of mission service in China passed before her in panoramic view.

She had been a young bride when they first came to China. One of the aims of the church in those days had been to build a clinic in Shanghai. First she learned the language, slowly, laboriously, but finally successfully. Then she received her assignment— to go out among the wealthy and raise funds to build the clinic. Her job was to contact them, present the plans, and enlist their aid.

God had blessed abundantly. Money flowed in from every direction. Rich Chinese willingly contributed, many of them in the same class as Low Sing. Now the tall building located on Range Road stood as a monument to their generosity. By the end of the first year more than fifty thousand of Shanghai's poorest had passed through its doors.

John's work took him out of town often. Olga discovered that loneliness and separation from her husband were part of the price a missionary wife pays for the privilege of service overseas. But her life was always full.

One of the satisfactions of those early years had been the feeding of the hungry who daily came to the mission. The mission workers had put up across the street from the compound a crude shed made of bamboo mats. Here they ladled out rice and beans to the endless lines. In some cases they were able to provide cloth also for the destitute.

One particular scene stood out—the day when 3,000 children came and formed a pathetic line of malnutrition. Bowl after bowl of rice was passed out, until at last the big copper kettle was empty.

Then emaciated parents came, and more children. Leaning against the compound walls, they had begged for food. Mission officials filled with helpless compassion had been compelled to say, "We are sorry, but there is no more rice. No more food of any kind." But the people would not leave.

"We cannot help you," staff workers repeated. "You must not stay here against the walls of the compound."

"No!" came the voices. "We will not leave. You have given our children food. Now you must feed us too. If you cannot, we will die at your door."

The police, finally, had been compelled to lead them away. How she and John had grieved to watch the hungry and wretched poor forcibly dispersed because the rice bin was empty.

Life in China was cheap. She remembered how babies, if they were girl babies born to the beggarly, never saw the light of day. Desperate, hungry mothers pinched the infant's nostrils, snuffing out the breath of life, rather than doom the baby to a life of slow starvation. And it was common practice for parents to sell their little girls, called "slaves," into a life of servitude for a paltry sum of money.

Even in the Adventist clinic the nurses had to guard the new-born babies, lest their mothers pinch away their breath.

Now, against the backdrop of this poverty and need, Olga reviewed this most recent episode and her refusal to comply with Low Sing's request. She wondered again if she had done the right thing. She believed she had, but still she could not help wishing that Low Sing's wealth, as well as he himself, could have been utilized in feeding and clothing the needy and in bringing healing to the sick. And most of all, that Low Sing and his mother could have found in Christ not only temporal assurance, which they so desperately sought, but also eternal life.

But like the rich young ruler who came to Jesus but went away clinging to his wealth, Low Sing's whole concern was his money, and he soon perished with it. The tragic sequel to his story Olga heard the next day from friends of Low Sing's family.

In the afternoon of the day Low Sing and his mother left Olga, they boarded a coastal steamer headed south to Foochow. Determined that they would flee before the enemy struck and that no one would take their wealth, Low Sing carried on his person the thousands of dollars' worth of diamonds.

The steamer had hardly gone halfway down the coast when a dreaded typhoon struck without warning. The crew fought desperately against the raging elements, but in vain. Finally losing the battle against the driving rain and unrelenting wind, the ship with all its crew and wealthy passengers fleeing the city of Shanghai went down.

Low Sing, his family, and his treasured diamonds were lost forever.

John Oss upon his belated return heard the complete and almost incredible story. "You made the right decision, dear," he assured his wife. "But what a tragedy that Low Sing could not have known of Jesus' love and found in Him a sure refuge! How differently his story might have ended if he had been acquainted with Christ's teachings, especially with the parable of the rich man who made the mistake of storing up his possessions on earth."

Looking sad, John Oss continued, "Had Low Sing realized when he came here to ask you to hide the diamonds that the next day *his* soul would be required of him, I wonder what he would have done?"

The Bombs Fall— December 8, 1941

December 8, 1941

The hot winds of war continued to fan the air. At every turn John and Olga witnessed fear and horror among the people, and the hasty preparations on the part of many to flee the city.

While she and John waited for the inevitable, Olga could not push aside her own feelings of premonition. Turning to John one evening as he was searching through some papers, she asked, "John, what will we do when the war starts? Where will we go?" Looking at his calm face, she marveled at his tranquil spirit, but was thankful that her husband was a man of steady, unchanging faith.

Suddenly the telephone rang. Olga hurried to answer. It was Dr. Dale calling from the Shanghai Sanitarium. Both the tone of his voice and what he said alarmed Olga, sending quivers up and down her spine.

"Oh no—it can't be—not this soon!" she managed to say, and then dropped into the little chair next to the telephone stand. John had followed her into the hallway and sensed at once that something serious had happened.

"That was Dr. Dale from the sanitarium," Olga informed him. "He's picked up the war news on his short wave radio. The Japanese fleet is swarming all over the Pacific. Part of it is headed for Shanghai—right here, John—and Hong Kong. Another part is headed for Honolulu. John, what shall we do now?"

John was silent. He seemed too stunned to answer.

"We're going to have to leave here quickly, aren't we?" Olga persisted.

"Olga, my dear, calm down. These may be just rumors."

"Rumors? Oh, no, John. Dr. Dale is serious. War will break out any minute now, and we may be wiped off the face of the earth."

Then the phone rang again and John picked up the receiver. Olga studied his face. "Yes, yes, Dr. Dale, we'll leave tomorrow in our houseboat. Thank you, doctor." Unruffled, he replaced the receiver and faced his wife.

"Dr. Dale says we mustn't wait any longer. The area is hot. He says we must leave early tomorrow morning."

Extending a hand to Olga, he said, "Come, dear. Let's think this thing out calmly. And let's trust our heavenly Father to guide us."

"All right, John, what shall we do first?" Olga tried to match her husband's calmness. "Where shall we go? How can we get away quickly?"

"Well, first we must get out our warmest clothing. We'll have to leave with only the clothes on our backs, you know." Olga nodded.

"But *where* will we go?" Her voice was unsteady.

"We'll take our houseboat. Old and dilapidated though it may be, it should take us down the canal and away from the city."

"Then where to?"

A faint smile met Olga's anxious eyes. "I guess to no-man's-land, darling. We'll travel by night."

"Won't the Japanese recognize us by our clothes? They'll know we are Americans."

"Without a doubt, if we don't disguise ourselves. We'll get some Chinese clothes and take a chance that they won't recognize us as Americans." John caressed his wife's blond tresses. "Let's see, I think we can braid your hair and give you a Chinese look," he teased a little. "And now, come, let's get some rest." Lights in most of the houses had already gone out.

As they walked into the bedroom, John wound the clock and

set the alarm. "There's no packing to do. We'll get up at four o'clock," he said as he tumbled into bed. "Don't stay up too late, dear," he added.

Olga, reluctant to go to bed, marveled at her husband's calm spirit. For her, brushing aside fear didn't come so easy. What would tomorrow bring? Would they ever see their homeland again?

She remembered her girlhood days back in Nebraska and her first years of married life. She was still a young bride when John had received the call for overseas mission service. They had accepted it, and for twenty-two years China had been their home.

China had always been a land plagued by war and poverty, and now it was threatened with an all-out conflict with Japan. Earlier, when this possibility had become more evident, it had been suggested that they leave China and return to America. They had considered the move, but in the end had decided to stay on. Now the fury of the times had broken upon them.

The noises of the night kept Olga from falling asleep. She prayed as she listened. "Dear God, Thou hast directed our paths and protected us for twenty-two years. Show us now where we must go and what we must do tomorrow." Finally, however, exhaustion overcame her and she, too, fell asleep.

It was exactly four a.m. when Olga was awakened by a double blast—first that of the alarm clock and then the rat-a-tat-tat of distant machine guns.

Instantly Olga was out of bed peering through the curtains. Lights flickered in every direction. Suddenly the city blazed like the rays of the sun at high noon. John, still asleep, had not stirred. Olga dashed back to the bed and shook him. "John, John, the war has started! We're too late! Wake up."

John moved a little.

"Please, John, wake up. Don't you understand? The Japanese guns have gone off. The war is on. Get up." She ran for her clothes.

"Olga, go back to sleep. This isn't war. It's probably just ban-

2—B.B.W.

dits blowing up something." He didn't even realize the alarm had gone off.

Olga selected their warmest clothing. "Here are your clothes. Please, dear, hurry. We can't stay here another minute." In no time Olga was fully dressed, ready for immediate departure. It was hard to keep the tears back. They certainly hadn't expected the guns to start this soon!

The ringing of the phone caused John finally to sit up in bed and reach for his clothes.

Olga had already picked up the receiver. "Yes, Dr. Dale," she almost shouted into the receiver.

The doctor's voice came loud and clear. "Olga, now listen to me. The war has started. The news just came over the radio. The Japanese have bombed Hong Kong, Singapore, and Honolulu. I'm starting out right away for Rubicon Road. I'll meet you and John at the sanitarium. You must get out NOW. Hurry, don't wait another minute."

"Yes, yes, we'll meet you there right away," Olga answered.

By this time John had slipped into his clothes, spurred by the excitement in his wife's voice. He met her in the hallway. Alarm showed on Olga's face. "John, the war has *really* started. Dr. Dale says we should leave now and meet him at the sanitarium."

John placed an arm around his wife. " 'Thou shalt not be afraid for the terror by night,' " he quoted. His calm support did something for her. Almost instantly she relaxed and managed a weak smile.

Looking around the room, Olga wondered what else besides the clothes on their backs they could take. Turning to John she asked, "How will we travel the fourteen miles to the sanitarium without being caught?"

Before he could reply, the phone rang again and John went running to answer. "All right, sir. We'll try to do that." He slipped the receiver gently back on its hook.

"Who was that, John?" Olga wanted to know.

"The American consul. He wants us to get within their concession as soon as possible. He said we must also burn any papers that might incriminate us. You get all the letters while I start a fire. We'll leave as soon as we have burned them." John walked into the dining room and soon was stoking a fire in the stove.

Olga brought all the letters from friends in the United States, letters from Chinese friends, and letters from mission headquarters. Without hestitation she flung them into the stove. John stirred the fire so that the flames would consume every scrap.

Suddenly Olga remembered something. "John, what about the payroll money?" Entrusted to their care the day before by the mission treasurer was $20,000 in silver which would go to pay the 600 workers of the Shanghai Sanitarium.

"That's right, Olga." John paused for a moment. "We can't take it with us. We must leave it in the locker and trust our heavenly Father to take care of His own."

Olga thought about their Chinese friends. Perhaps they could take charge of the money. "Do you think we ought to call our friends and tell them about it?"

"No!" John's answer was emphatic. "The invaders may be tapping the wires."

At that moment the door slid open, and their servant Su Deh and her husband Hung Bin came running into the room. Alarm was written on their faces too, which only intensified Olga's fear. They offered to help with anything they could.

Just then the phone rang again. Olga fairly leaped into the hallway. As she was about to lift the receiver, she pushed aside the curtains that hung above the phone stand and looked out into the street beyond the six-foot wall that circled the mission compound. What she saw horrified her. An army truck was screeching to a halt before the compound. Under the street lights that illuminated the area she followed the scene—like watching a drama on a stage.

A Japanese soldier sat in the cab. Behind him stood two more soldiers. The door opened quickly, and the soldier jumped out and started toward the compound gate. She saw that he was dressed in full army uniform and carried in his hand a rifle with bayonet attached. On his head he wore a steel helmet. The clump of his feet utterly unnerved her.

While the phone continued to ring Olga stood galvanized on the spot. But finally she managed to lift the receiver. Over the wires came the voice of Dr. Dale. "Hello, hello. Olga—John— are you there?"

Her lips formed a weak, "Yes, Charles."

"Olga, this is Dr. Dale. Listen to me. It's too late. None of us can escape. Every bridge in the city is now guarded by the invading forces."

For a few seconds fresh panic silenced Olga's voice. Then she whispered. "Well, Charles, it's too late for us, anyhow. Enemy soldiers have come for us. They're here right now, just outside the gate. This is the end."

Even as she spoke the soldier was nearing the gate. And now she remembered with added consternation that they had forgotten to lock it last night. A paralyzing constriction around her heart took her breath away. She watched the soldier reach for the latch, fumble a few seconds, and come in. Olga noted the neat row of cartridges that circled his belt.

Forcing herself to move, she found herself shutting the sliding door between the hallway and the dining room where John was still working the fire. If she were going to be killed, John must not be a witness. She returned to the phone, feeling her knees bending. Dr. Dale was still on the line; she could hear his heavy breathing. "Charles, pray for us. Our time has come!" she whispered into the mouthpiece.

The thumping of the soldier's boots came closer. Under the street lights his facial features were clearly visible. And the bayonet, held high in his hand, glittered in the moonlight as he moved toward the front door.

The Bombs Fall—December 8, 1941

"Good-bye, Charles, he's here." The phone slipped to the floor. Olga fell to her knees. "Oh, God," she prayed. "Give me strength to face this death. And don't let John see me die. Make it quick. Thou art my strength and my Redeemer." The horror of it almost made her faint. "Please, God," she pleaded, "let it be fast."

3 | The Escape

Olga shut her eyes. From the receiver on the floor the voice of Dr. Dale sounded muffled though clear. "Olga, Olga, now listen. Be calm. Remember that He who is with you is greater than he who is against you."

Olga heard. If only her heart would stop now, before the soldier killed her. Instead it boomed a steady rhythm. She could think of only one thing. John must *not* see her die.

Determined that John must not see or hear, she stifled the scream that tried to escape her throat. And she waited. What was keeping the enemy that had come to take their lives? Why was he taking so long? Opening her eyes, she observed the soldier still moving, rifle in hand. But what she saw next made her leap to her feet. The soldier was now walking *away* from the house, back toward the truck. She could hardly believe her eyes! And upon reaching it he jumped in and drove away.

Olga sank to the floor. "Thank You, God," she whispered, palms moist with perspiration. Oh, this awful weakness! She must collect herself and go to John. God had spared her life. Perhaps there was still time to escape. Pulling herself to her feet, she opened the door. John was still stoking the fire. Seeing her face, he exclaimed, "Why, Olga, whatever is wrong?" Noting her weakness, he placed a supporting arm around her waist.

"John, let's get out of this house. Now! This minute! Japanese soldiers were here with their guns and bayonets. One of them opened the gate and came into our yard." Olga spoke in a horrified whisper.

John led his wife to a chair. "Here, sit down. Yes, yes, now tell me exactly what happened." Grave concern covered his face.

"I saw the soldier come straight up the path with his rifle and bayonet in his hand. He seemed to be looking for a number. Then —then, suddenly, when I looked again, he seemed to change his mind about something, and—and—" Her voice faltered, as though she could hardly believe her own words. "Then, he walked away."

John knelt and held her closely. "My darling, God has indeed spared our lives, and He will guide us now. We must be true witnesses for Him. And we must leave here at once before they come looking for us again." He helped her to her feet, and Olga was glad for his steadiness.

As they readied themselves to leave, an idea flashed into Olga's mind. "John," she said, "I have an idea. Why don't we go to the house of our friends, the Ollenstopps? They're Swiss, and the invaders won't bother them. They're neutral! We'll hide, and they won't find us." Olga brightened now that a ray of hope had come into her heart. "Surely they won't object, since they are among our best friends."

"Olga, that's a wonderful idea," John beamed. At least it was a temporary solution to their problem of where to go. He was sure they wouldn't mind. However, disturbing friends this early in the morning seemed to concern him. "They may still be asleep," he said.

"We'll wake them up," Olga replied.

"All right. Come on, let's go."

Leaving the $20,000 mission payroll money, and forgetting their passports, the Osses left their comfortable mission home and started for the Ollenstopp residence one block down the street. Though the darkness of night still lingered, they walked briskly. Suddenly within the dusky shadows Olga spotted a man crouching. Fresh panic gripped her. Then the man began to move slowly in their direction, and it seemed to Olga that he carried a bayonet in his hands. Clutching her husband's arm, she whispered, "Let's run."

Placing a firm arm around his wife, John warned, "Olga, don't you *dare* run. Walk slowly." Only his firm support kept her from falling to the ground in her weakness.

Only a few yards before them the treetops and walls around the Ollenstopps' residence formed a silhouette. John said, "Steady now, we're almost there." To Olga it seemed miles. She was sure the crouching soldier would kill them before they could get there. John held her back. But finally they stood before the scrolled gate. Olga was aware that something John did brought a slow-moving servant to hover around the gate. Why didn't he hurry? Without warning, then, she felt her knees buckle under her, and everything went dark.

When she opened her eyes again, she found herself resting in a clean white bed in the home of the Ollenstopps. Mrs. Ollenstopp held her hand and smiled sympathetically. "Poor dear! John told us all about your frightful ordeal. You fainted right on our concrete steps. Of course you may both stay here. Our home is your home now."

"Yes," added Mr. Ollenstopp, "if necessary, we can hide you in the factory next door. I don't believe the Japanese would ever search for you in our loom plant."

Gratitude filled Olga's heart. John Oss looked into his wife's blue eyes and smiled. "Olga," he said, "you need not have worried about the man you saw in the street. He was only a Chinese coolie, and when we stopped beside the gate, he walked right past us." Then turning to his hosts, he asked to use their phone. "I must try to get through to mission headquarters," he explained.

"Yes, of course, you must inform the mission authorities of your whereabouts," replied Mr. Ollenstopp.

John informed the men at the office that they had had to flee and that they had been compelled to leave the $20,000 payroll money in the locker of their home. Also that in their haste they had forgotten to take their passports.

Before the morning sun could flood the sky with light, Pastor

Hsu Hwa, an important leader of the work in China, and S. J. Lee, secretary-treasurer of the Shanghai branch committee, were on their way across town to the house once occupied by the Osses. They were well aware that any American in sight would be public enemy number one for the Japanese. Of course the Chinese, too, were thoroughly despised by them, but the city of Shanghai was already a conquered city. And though it was heavily patrolled and guarded by the occupation forces, every Chinese patriot was, for the most part, an unmolested prisoner at large.

Reaching the house, they were able to retrieve the payroll money and the passports. They returned, however, to report to the Osses that already their house had been ransacked. Looters had lost no time in stealing clothes, furniture, and even Olga's purse and loose money. They were sure that only God's protection had prevented them from finding the payroll money.

Olga and John felt that possibly the looting was the work of servants who reasoned that it was better for them to take their master's possessions rather than to let the enemy seize everything.

"But thank God, they didn't find the payroll money. The sanitarium workers can be paid tomorrow," John said gratefully.

Mrs. Ollenstopp kindly urged Olga to remain in bed and rest. When, around nine o'clock, a servant brought her some food, Olga could not swallow a bite. John, too, could not eat. Sitting on the edge of his wife's bed, he comforted her by saying, "Things are not as bad as they appear, Olga, and I want you to relax now and stop worrying. We are completely in God's hands."

Olga nodded. "I know, dear. God is surely our strength now. But," she smiled weakly, "I thought for sure they were going to kill us in cold blood."

"Of course you had a terrible experience, but now forget it and let's trust our heavenly Father. We are in safe hands. Try to rest. I'll be back in a little while." He tucked the covers around her and left.

It was ten o'clock when Olga again heard John's soft footsteps in the room. The unusually serious look on his face caused her to sit up. "John, something's happened, hasn't it?"

Quietly John addressed his wife, "Now, Olga, you will have to get up. They're here."

Before he could explain, Olga guessed what he meant. "The Japanese are here, aren't they?"

John nodded, still unruffled. "Now keep calm, dear. These men are not Japanese soldiers—only civilian officers dressed like Japanese gentlemen. In fact, they're dressed Western style in nice black suits. You won't be afraid of them. They're government trained, very courteous, not at all belligerent. But they have a job to do."

John looked so undisturbed. Again Olga felt his wonderful strength. "But what do they want?"

"Well, I don't know, but they want to see both of us. Come on now, just walk quietly beside me." He took her hand and led her into the living room where the Japanese officials stood waiting. At the sight of these men Olga again felt weak all over. Though dressed in American-style clothing, they were still the enemy.

One official stepped forward and addressed them in remarkably good English. "You are now Japanese prisoners of war. You are at all times in grave danger. We will, however, protect you"— a giant smile lined his face—"if you obey our orders implicitly. But—" He paused and spoke deliberately. "If you try to escape, the Japanese government cannot protect you." Taking a notebook from his pocket he wrote. "You must report any change of location you make. And you must not attempt to leave the city. You could be shot on sight. You will receive orders from the Japanese government, and until then, do not make a move."

The other official stepped forward and held out two armbands carrying the numbers 842 and 843. Handing one to each of the Osses he added his warning, "You must wear these armbands at all times, wherever you appear."

John nodded his head courteously. Olga burst out with, "Oh, yes, yes, we will cooperate."

"Good!" The civilian officer seemed pleased. Olga noted the rigid crease of his black pants. On the surface, at least, he appeared to be a gentleman, though she was confident that not an ounce of mercy would he show should they violate his orders.

After they left, Olga was first to find her tongue. "How did they know we were here, and why did they seize us now?"

John replied, "In answer to your first question, I don't know, and secondly, let's face it. They are just biding time. We are prisoners at large for the time being. We will, eventually, be interned." He held up the armband that labeled him prisoner number 842. "These armbands will indicate that we are prisoners of the Japanese."

Silently Olga offered thanks to God for the little reprieve they now had before being flung into a Japanese prison camp.

For the next three days John and Olga, fearing to roam the war-tense city, stayed inside their friends' home. On the third day Dr. Dale called to tell them that, somehow, he had managed to reach the sanitarium and for the time being would stay there. He had learned their whereabouts and the story of God's providential care over them from the office workers at the mission.

On the fourth day a report came that all Americans and British would be allowed liberty only within the limits of the International Settlement and the French concession. Registration, passes, and periodical questionings would be required at all times. Deciding that they no longer needed to impose on their friends, the Ollenstopps, John and Olga hired a cart and went to the French concession, where they found a room in a boardinghouse.

The first night Olga felt something crawling all over the bed. "John, let's turn on the lights," she urged. A flick of the switch, and the creeping things were exposed.

"Bedbugs!" cried Olga. "Hundreds of them. Oh, John, how can we sleep in this bed?" Olga jumped out of bed and stood there shuddering in her nightclothes. The bed was simply alive, and bloodstains covered the sheets. Olga felt she could endure many hardships, if need be, but bed companionship with countless bed-bugs was not one of them.

Shaking his head at the crawling turn of events, John said patiently, "We'll find another room tomorrow."

The next day they found an empty cottage on Yuen Road in International Settlement and obtained permission from the Japanese to occupy it. Here they received unexpected kind attention. Two young Chinese girls, friends of the Osses from the Shanghai Sanitarium, volunteered to come out and be their helpers until the time came for them to be interned.

As John and Olga moved about cautiously, they discovered that the red armbands brought fear to some of the merchants. Entrance to the theaters, restaurants, parks, and public places was positively forbidden, and supplies became hard to obtain.

Although John and Olga remained close to the cottage, there were times when they had to make short trips to the stores. One morning, walking into a market, Olga begged a merchant to sell her some soap.

"Oh, no. You enemy, and must not be seen here. Go." The fearful Chinese merchant pushed her out of the market.

Another time, a little Japanese girl, playing in the street with a wooden bayonet, poked Olga in the stomach. It soon became evident that no Japanese would miss an opportunity to spit at them. John and Olga decided it was best not to venture unnecessarily into the streets.

In spite of the hostile attitude they encountered, John and Olga braved a walk one afternoon to bid adieu to some of their Chinese friends. As they passed the Hong Kong Tailor Shop, John remembered that when he had purchased his clothes there, the Chinese with whom he had dealt had been most friendly and courteous. How would they feel now toward them? From the window it seemed that their friends had spotted them, for one of them came running out saying, "Come in! come in!" The red armbands did not seem to disturb them. Seeing his friendliness,

John and Olga eagerly accepted the invitation and stepped inside the shop.

"Oh, we are so happy to see you, Mr. and Mrs. Oss." The man bowed politely. Glancing significantly at the telltale armbands, he spoke most sympathetically. "We know you have done much to help our people. You have been wonderful friends of the Chinese. Now—now it is our turn to help you."

Olga and John looked at each other in amazement. After all the hostility, such kindness came as a mild shock. Olga smiled at their rotund friend. "You are so kind. But we are prisoners of war. To help us would be dangerous and might get you in trouble."

"Yes, yes, we know you are prisoners of war. But we have many friends. We will combine together and place some money in the bank of Shanghai for both of you," offered their wonderful benefactor. "You may use it whenever you need it."

Now John could not keep silent. Although they had been deprived of clothes, furniture, and their home, God in His mercy had spared their lives. They could not, however, accept money from these loyal friends. He turned to his friend. "We are most grateful for your kindness in wanting to help us, and while we cannot accept money, perhaps you could help us by procuring food supplies and other necessities for us."

"Oh, of course, we will help most gladly." The Chinese face became a wreath of smiles.

True to his promise, their friend appealed to other friends, and under cover of darkness these kind people supplied them with all kinds of provisions. Food, and even sugar—a very scarce item— and soap were made available to them. And although John and Olga offered to repay them someday, they refused to accept any payment.

Japanese officials kept in close touch with the Osses and advised them, "Soon you will be interned in a camp and will be allowed one forty-pound package of food and supplies per month. This must be handled by your Swiss contacts." Later the Japanese changed their minds and would allow only twenty pounds per month. There would be no soap or sundry items available at camp, so the Osses would have to depend on their friends to send them these supplies.

As this word spread around, other Chinese friends came to the rescue. Packages containing food and staples were secured, prepared, and stored in attics ready for the time when they could be shipped to the camp. Friends promised to keep sending them regularly, for they knew not what conditions awaited the Americans at the prison camp.

Weeks slipped by while John and Olga waited for the day of internment. Visions of cruelties at the hands of the enemy persisted in flashing onto Olga's mental screen. But always John's fervent prayers, his quiet faith, and unruffled spirit were a source of inspiration to her.

At last the day came in February when one of their helpers, Louise, came running into the room where John and Olga seemed to spend an eternal vigil. "Elder Oss, you are wanted on the telephone next door," she announced excitedly.

When John returned, Olga knew instantly from the noncommittal but serious look on his face that the dreaded time had come. Her eyes pleaded with her husband to say it wasn't so. She did not want to believe that the time had come for them to be incarcerated. She shook her head in opposition. "No, John," she said.

John's eyes wanted to comfort her, but the words came quietly, "Yes, dear. The time has come. We leave next Thursday for prison camp."

A Coffin and the Twenty-third Psalm | 4

The Japanese government had ordered all Americans in Shanghai to meet at the Columbia Country Club. From there they were to be taken in buses to the prison camp. This was the information John had received, and which he now conveyed to his wife.

From the kitchen, the girls Louise and Betty, still eating lunch, overheard. A moment later, without a word of explanation, they left the table and rushed past the Osses out the back door. "What's the matter with the girls?" John asked.

Olga shrugged her shoulders. But when they heard loud wails from the outside, they knew. The girls had heard the news, and their hearts were broken. They wept for hours in spite of the Osses' efforts to comfort them.

After the first impact of John's announcement, Olga became unusually pensive. Somehow, now that the time for internment had actually arrived, she felt empty of all emotion. Even fear had vanished. Faith in God was stronger than ever. "The Lord is my strength. Whom shall I fear?" kept running through her mind.

As always, she turned to John for direction. "John, what do we need to do first?" she asked.

"We must first go down to American Association Headquarters. There we will be given a list of things we must take along. Time is short. Let's go now."

At headquarters, which had been organized for the purpose of furnishing information to Americans in Shanghai, they were given the list. It included a number of housekeeping items as beds, bedding, tableware, cooking pans, towels, and clothing for warm and cold weather. Also sundry items such as scissors, hand mirrors, clothes hangers, can openers, needles and thread, safety pins, buttons, hot-water bottles, ashtrays, et cetera. And they were told that none of these items would be supplied at camp. The Japanese government would permit packages from friends once a month— only one per month. These must not weigh more than twenty pounds.

With only four days left, John and Olga hastened back to their little cottage, and packed as many items as they could take along. Then with the help of their Chinese friends they also packed additional supplies into twenty-pound packages, ready to be sent to them in future days.

Since they were soon to leave for camp, Olga felt impressed to visit some special friends and say good-bye. First would be John Way, whose palatial home was near the French concession not far from their cottage. This man was a fabulously wealthy merchant who had contributed generously and regularly through the years to the Adventist sanitarium in Shanghai. Olga had met him first many years before at the Shanghai Sanitarium, and he had remained a good friend to John and her ever since.

Taking her Bible, Olga started off by herself, red armband in full view. Walking briskly, she soon arrived before the beautifully hand-carved gate that opened into a beautiful court. She paused a moment, and almost immediately a servant appeared. Speaking in broken English, he asked, "You have card, please?" He bowed. Olga of course knew the custom of showing one's identification card before gaining admission to a wealthy home. But did she have one? For an embarrassed moment she fumbled in her purse. Sure enough, she did. She showed it to the servant, who left and returned a few moments later with John Way himself.

In the meantime, Olga stood taking in the beauty of the landscaped garden around her. Flowers and trees blended together to make a heavenly picture.

John Way greeted her with genuine pleasure; yet somehow, Olga detected a look of deep sadness on his handsome face.

"Mrs. Oss, oh, I am so glad you have come." He glanced at her armband, and his face showed regret. "My wife is very ill. She has tuberculosis, and cannot live much longer." The words came in flawless English.

"Oh, I am so very sorry to hear that, Mr. Way." Wanting to comfort him, she was prompted to reply, "But we have a God in heaven who knows all our problems and hears our prayers."

John Way's eyes remained heavy with sadness. "Mrs. Oss, would you please pray for my wife? I love her very much and don't want her to die. Would you please come in and see her?"

"Why, yes, I would love to." The gentleman's sorrow touched her, and she wished she could do something to comfort him.

John Way led Olga up a staircase, carpeted with a thick plush runner. Her hands rested on the intricately wrought black iron rail. John Way stopped before a beautiful door, polished to look like a mirror. "Please go in," he invited and walked softly away. It was evident that he wanted Olga to have a few moments alone with his sick wife. Olga entered a room of the most dazzling splendor. Each wall was fully paneled with expensive mirrors. Lustrous tapestries of iridescent colors hung here and there throughout the room. Pieces of ivory and bronze and exquisitely designed vases decorated every corner of the room. Every square inch spelled elegance beyond description.

On the bed, wearing a flowing gown of pure silk and resting on sheets of crepe de chine, lay Mrs. John Way. Olga had heard that Mrs. Way was rated by many the most beautiful woman in Shanghai. Now Olga saw for herself. Tiny, and angelic white, she looked like a pure lily. Olga noticed her eyes—luminous black pools against a delicate face that seemed to possess an ethereal quality. A tiny smile crossed the lovely face.

As Olga smiled in return and looked at the tiny bit of fragile humanity, she sensed that here was a candle about to flicker out. As she introduced herself, an expression of recognition brightened Mrs. Way's face.

3—B.B.W.

Speaking in a soft, little-girl voice, Mrs. Way said, "My husband has told me about you and your husband, and I was wishing you would come." Each word came in flawless English. Olga recalled, too, that Mrs. Way had been graduated from an exclusive girls' school in Shanghai. Her English was most pleasant to Olga's Chinese-attuned ears.

Olga had the feeling that Mrs. Way knew her days were numbered. So she put all the warmth and sympathy she could muster into a smile for the woman at death's door. "Mrs. Way, I am so happy to meet you, but sad to find you ill."

"Yes," came the tiny whisper. "I fear my illness is—is—is—" Pain and fear filled the beautiful eyes, and suddenly she was crying softly into the silk sheets. Then lifting her head, she told Olga, "Mrs. Oss, I do not believe I shall ever rise from this bed." Fresh tears spilled on petal checks.

"Mrs. Way," Olga said gently, "do you mind if I pray to our God?"

The tear-stained face turned and faced Olga. She glanced at Olga's Bible. "Oh, please do." She even managed a wan smile.

Opening her Bible to the twenty-third psalm, Olga read in a clear, soft voice, " 'Yea, though I walk through the valley of the shadow of death, I will fear no evil: for Thou art with me; Thy rod and Thy staff they comfort me.' "

The tender face beamed. "Please, please, read that to me again."

Again Olga read, this time the entire psalm. The words seemed to bring comfort to Mrs. Way. "Will you tell me more about your God?"

Within the next few hours, the God of love, the God of Christianity, was introduced to the dying woman. And, Mrs. Way, on the threshold of eternity, feverishly drank of the words of life.

When Olga realized that hours had passed, she closed her Bible and rose to leave.

"Please come back tomorrow," whispered Mrs. Way. "I want to hear more about your God. I want to believe in Him."

She did not even look tired, but happy. "Will you come?"

"Yes, I will come again tomorrow," promised Olga, and with a smile passed quietly out of the room.

The next day she returned with a Bible for Mrs. Way. Together now they read God's promises. "Please read the twenty-third psalm for me again," begged the beautiful woman.

After Olga read it again, she noticed that something had brought distress to Mrs. Way. The sick lady's next words revealed what it was. "John said that you are leaving for prison camp very soon. Mrs. Oss, why did you not tell me?"

So that was why her friend was disturbed. "Well, I did not want to shock you," replied Olga.

Mrs. Way was silent, but only for a few seconds. "Do you realize that you may be killed by the Japanese?"

"Yes, Mrs. Way, I do."

"Are you not afraid?"

"No. The psalm says, 'Though I walk through the valley of the shadow of death, I will fear no evil: for Thou art with me.'" Olga spoke happily. She remembered how once she had been horrified. Now, somehow, all fear of death at the hands of the enemy had vanished. God had strengthened her faith and trust, and she felt that she had given her friend an honest reply.

Stretching out a tiny lily hand, Mrs. Way beckoned, "Please come closer, Mrs. Oss. I have something to tell you."

Olga clasped the hand of her friend. "Mrs. Oss, I know the truth about my illness. I know I am going to die, and very soon." While Olga felt her throat tightening, Mrs. Way smiled a beautiful smile and continued, "Before you came, I was terrified about dying. Now I am not. I believe in your God. I want to go to heaven. And I want to meet you there." Olga felt a weak pressure from Mrs. Way's hand. "Somehow, I feel that when you leave here today, I will never see you again. Not on this earth. But if I get to heaven, I will look for you there."

Listening to the words of her beautiful young friend and hearing her declare her newfound belief in the God of Christianity, kindled an emotion in Olga that she could never translate into words.

It made her think of the thief on the cross. Hadn't he said, "Lord, remember me when Thou comest into Thy kingdom?" Hadn't Christ at that very moment promised him Paradise? It was never too late for the God of Christianity.

"My dear, with God's help, I will be faithful. I want to see you in heaven too." Olga spoke from her heart and looked Mrs. Way directly in the eyes. "Now I must leave."

As Olga took her leave, she made a mental photograph of the peace and joy that glowed on Mrs. Way's face. She would carry it with her through the unknown darkness of the days ahead.

Downstairs in the living room, John Way waited for her. "Please sit down, Mrs. Oss." Olga sank into a silk-upholstered sofa. (Later she was to learn that the silken threads upon which she sat, formed the hiding place of $20,000 which John Way had hidden in anticipation of trouble. The money was found, however, by the Communists at a later time. John Way was imprisoned, and only a miracle saved him from death.)

"Mrs. Oss, may I ask a special favor of you?"

Without hesitation, Olga replied, "Why, of course."

John Way seemed relieved. "I ask this of you because of the great esteem I feel for you and your church. And what I ask of you must be done at once—this afternoon."

When Olga nodded, he continued, "I would like to have you select a coffin for my wife. I want her to have the very best. It must be airtight and waterproof. Get her one made in America."

Olga expressed no sign of surprise, for she was well acquainted with the Chinese custom of selecting a coffin before the day of death. It was not at all unusual to make a selection and park the box inside the home in preparation for the day of need. Often it was used as a place to sit. Olga remembered clearly the day she visited friends and was invited to sit on such a box, only to learn later that it contained the remains of the family's grandmother, and was awaiting a proper astrological day for burial.

Anxious to do all she could to spare John Way this sad and unpleasant duty, she replied quickly, "Certainly, Mr. Way. I will go right now."

John Way's chauffeur drove Olga to the International Funeral Parlor in Shanghai. There she met the owner, Mr. Scopp. Cordially he led her into a room adorned by the most impressive and expensive resting cases in the world.

"Here is one that is the exact match of Sun Yat-sen's," Mr. Scopp beamed.

Olga appreciated the reason for Mr. Scopp's personal pride in mentioning Sun Yat-sen, for he was revered in China like George Washington in America—the father of the republic of China.

Although price was no factor with Mr. Way, Olga's natural conservatism led her to ask, "How much does that one cost?"

Mr. Scopp was well acquainted with John Way's wealthy status. So he did not blink one eyelash when he replied, "$25,000. And it is *exactly* the same as the one in which Sun Yat-sen is buried at Purple Mountain in Nanking."

Somehow, Olga could not shake off the feeling that a deceased person could rest just as easily in something under $25,000. "Let me look at others, please," she requested.

"Of course." Mr. Scopp led her around to others; and after much viewing of resting cases, Olga found the one that seemed just right for Mrs. Way.

It was made of solid bronze, and imported from America. The surface, in the sunlight streaming from the window, dazzled the eye. Lacy tufts and soft white satin folds tumbled all about the interior. A soft pillow, intricately shirred, almost bid welcome. It did not take much stretch of the imagination to visualize the still form of Mrs. Way resting in this coffin.

"What is the price of this one?"

"Oh, that one is fairly inexpensive. Only $8,000." Mr. Scopp could not suppress his pleasure, for it was obvious Olga had made a choice.

"I will speak to Mr. Way about this one. I believe this is the one he will accept." Having made a decision, Olga did not want to waste a moment longer looking at the glorious furniture of the departed. Quickly she headed for the door.

The waiting chauffeur drove her back to the home of John Way, who waited for her. She described to him the coffin that Mr. Scopp showed her first—the expensive one. "But I did not feel that that was just right for your wife," she explained.

"Mrs. Oss, I do not mind paying $25,000, but if you feel the other is more appropriate, then I will buy it." He seemed greatly relieved and grateful to Olga for taking care of the matter in his behalf. "Thank you, thank you, Mrs. Oss. Now is there anything you would like us to do for you before you leave for camp?" he asked.

Olga remembered that a few weeks before, after the Japanese had ordered them confined, he had given her and John a couple of decent beds with innerspring mattresses. Now, on an optimistic note, she made a request that she would soon afterward regret. "Our friends at the clinic have promised to give us some cots to take to camp. We would like to leave our good beds with you until we are released."

"Very good. Bring them over, and also anything else you wish to entrust to us. And, Mrs. Oss," he lowered his voice, "when my wife dies, I will have a message for you in the obituary column in the newspaper."

Olga expressed surprise. "Do you really think the Japanese will allow any newspapers to be circulated in camp?"

"I believe they will allow the *North China Daily News,* at least for a little while. Please watch the obituaries."

"All right." Olga promised.

With sadness on his handsome face, John Way bade Olga

good-bye. Curling his fingers and locking his hands together, he shook them in the customary manner of the Chinese.

With a heavy heart Olga shook her own hands the same way and left for the little cottage, anxious to tell John about the strange events of the day.

5 | The Enemy Hatchet Strikes

The morning of their last day before departure to camp Olga woke up with an uneasy feeling. For some reason she couldn't shake off the idea that this day she should make one more special visit. A valued friend, Tong Shioa Yi, or Mr. Tong, as he was called, was one of China's high government officials. Also known as an elder statesman, Mr. Tong was an indefatigable friend of the poor. He carried heavily the burden of China's poverty and crime.

Olga recalled with a rush of gratitude how instrumental he had been in helping to raise funds for the mission hospital and clinic. First, he had written a personal check for $10,000 when Olga had called on him. Then, even more important, he had given her valuable letters of introduction to wealthy merchants and people of prominence who could contribute. Because of his influence many thousands of dollars had flowed into the fund.

Olga had gone to him often to solicit his help and had always found him faultlessly kind and respectful, never weary of her requests in behalf of the poor and unfortunate. It was a pleasure to converse with him. He spoke flawless and fluent English. And no wonder. Mr. Tong was a graduate of one of America's greatest universities. His unusual warmth and courtesy made her feel most welcome.

She smiled to herself when she recalled that in spite of his many virtues, Mr. Tong exercised all the liberties accorded the typical man of wealth and nobility in China. It was his privilege to desire, acquire, and maintain as many wives as he could afford. She almost chuckled aloud when she recalled the last conversation they had had together in his palatial home.

"Mrs. Oss," he had said, "there is a young woman whom I love dearly and wish for a wife. She is my niece's friend." He had looked as pleased as a teen-ager.

Olga was aquainted with the young woman, but she could not hide her feeling of shock. "But, Mr. Tong, she is only a young girl." Mr. Tong was at that time approaching seventy and already had seven wives and forty-two children. It would hardly be polite to remind him of these details, so she did not know what else to say.

"Yes, I know," the elderly gentleman conceded. "But that doesn't matter. She loves me too and wants to marry me." Smiling with pride, his face assured her that it was quite all right. It was *not* all right, but how could *she* tell him?

Not long after that, Mr. Tong took the young woman to be his eighth bride. When Olga saw him again for some reason, he declared, "Mrs. Oss, this woman will be my last wife. I promise." Perhaps he felt that this promise would relieve her.

Now months had passed since she had seen him. Remembering that he lived on the Rue Ferguson in the French concession and not too far away, she decided to visit him before they left for prison camp. Dressing rather hurriedly because she felt that time was fast slipping by, she called to John, who was shaving, "John, I'm going to visit Mr. Tong today."

"Mr. Tong?" John replied. "Oh, yes, a good idea. He's that elder statesman with eight wives, isn't he?"

"Yes, he has eight wives," Olga said resignedly. Then she brightened. "Today I'm going to take Mr. Tong a Bible. He reads English perfectly. Perhaps he will discover how wrong it is to have eight wives!"

"Let's hope," John said as he rinsed his face.

Promising that she would not be gone too long, Olga took an old bicycle that a friend had lent them and pedaled off toward the Rue Ferguson. When she reached the black, scrolled gate flanked by two dragons, a servant came and allowed her to enter. After showing her into the reception room, plush with lustrous tapestries and furniture, he went to call Mr. Tong.

Her host appeared at once and seeing Olga, his face broke into a warm smile. Extending his hand, American fashion, he greeted, "How nice to see you, Mrs. Oss." His eye caught the red armband she wore. Instantly he became aware that she was a prisoner at large of the Japanese. The smile faded from his face.

"How is your husband, Mrs. Oss? And when will you leave for the Japanese prison camp?" he asked, most solicitously.

"John is fine, Mr. Tong. I have come to tell you good-bye. We leave for camp tomorrow."

Mr. Tong waved a ringed hand. His gesture invited her to be seated on one of the silk couches.

"And how is young Mrs. Tong?" Olga referred, of course, to wife number eight.

Mr. Tong beamed with pleasure. "I have some good news for you. My wife and I are expecting our first child. Perhaps he will be born on my seventieth birthday."

"How nice, Mr. Tong," Olga said politely. She was well aware of how much another son, if the baby were a boy, would mean to him, even if he were number forty-three.

Suddenly a sober look flashed across his face. Bending toward her, he lowered his voice to a confidential tone. "Mrs. Oss, the Japanese officials were here to talk with me."

Olga's heart jumped. "When—and why?"

"Recently. They offered me the premiership of China. Under their flag." Bitterness crept into his tone.

"But, Mr. Tong, why you?" Olga was shocked and afraid.

"Because I am so well acquainted with the affairs of the Chinese government."

Olga nodded her head in agreement. The news left her stunned. Collecting herself she spoke. "And—did—did you?"

"No, no. I did not accept. They offered me $10,000 a month. But I would rather die a poor man, if necessary, than to be a traitorous collaborator with the Japanese." A black bitterness showed in his voice. "I'll never accept a premiership for a puppet government."

For a moment Olga could say nothing. An awful dread had begun to seize her.

Seeing her disturbance, Mr. Tong attempted to distract her. "Mrs. Oss, I'm sorry you and your husband must leave so soon. My daughter is getting married, and we would have loved to have you attend the wedding."

"I'm sorry too." Chinese weddings were fabulous affairs when wealth and prestige were involved.

"The gifts have been arriving for days," continued Mr. Tong.

While he talked about the wedding, Olga reached into her small briefcase and pulled out a Bible. "Mr. Tong, I came here today with a purpose," she began. "As a Christian, I believe that the affairs of this earth are governed by our God. And this Bible—God's Book—tells us that in the not-too-distant future Jesus the Son of God will return to this earth and there will be a resurrection of the just. This world will be made new, and sin and sorrow and sickness and death will be no more."

Mr. Tong seemed to be interested and listened politely. "Please go on," he invited, twisting the few hairs on his chin.

"Mr. Tong, I'm truly sorry that I have not spoken to you before on this subject. I want you to have this Bible. It contains God's messages to His people. Please keep it and read it." She handed him the black, leather-bound Book.

Mr. Tong accepted the Bible and held it between his hands. "I thank you, Mrs. Oss," he said kindly. "And I promise to read it." His words had a ring of sincerity.

"I must leave now." Olga rose. "As I said, we are leaving for prison camp tomorrow and—and—perhaps I will never see you again." Sadness filled her voice.

Mr. Tong reached for her hand and for a second held it tightly.

"Good-bye, Mrs. Oss. May the God you believe in smile graciously upon you."

Moments later Olga left the house.

Hardly had she arrived back inside her own apartment when a voice from without, full of panic and urgency called, "Mrs. Oss! Mrs. Oss!" Running to the door, she discovered that it was a runner—a servant of Mr. Tong's household. His breath came in huge gulps. And on his face he wore a look of sheer agony and terror. Tears streamed along the wrinkles.

"What is it? What is it? Tell me quickly, man," Olga urged. Obviously something dreadful had happened—something too horrible for words—judging from the look on the man's face.

For a second the servant stopped shaking and tried to collect himself. But when he tried to talk again, sobs choked the words and he became incoherent.

"Please, man, please pull yourself together, and tell me quickly what happened." The man slipped to the floor from sheer weakness. Olga knelt beside him, afraid he was going to faint.

"Has something happened to Mr. Tong?" Her voice rose with excitement.

The man raised his face and the sobs slowed down. "Right after you were let out of the house the next people to arrive were two men—Chinese civilians." A prolonged sob almost choked the next sentence. "They carried expensive vases for Mr. Tong's daughter—her wedding presents." Suddenly the man's head dropped to his chest and fresh horror seemed to paralyze his speech.

Olga felt like wringing her own hands in desperation. "Please, man—then what happened?" She placed a hand on his shoulder.

"They—they insisted that they wanted Mr. Tong to sign a receipt for the vases." More sobs shook the poor man.

"Yes, go on—" A terrible dread surged through her veins.

"Then—then—then—" Sobs continued to convulse his body. "One man pulled a hatchet out of one of the vases—and—and—and hit Mr. Tong over the head—and killed him instantly." Now the man wept without control.

Wave after wave of horror passed through Olga.

Mr. Tong was dead—dead! Only moments before she had been with him, inspired by his warmth, courage, and loyalty for his people. Now he was dead. No doubt the two Chinese had been hired by the Japanese government to retaliate because he would not turn traitor and accept the premiership under their command.

Tears flowed freely down her face. Inside she was sick. Aloud she said, "Mr. Tong was the best friend we had in China. And now he's dead." Suddenly a sense of sharp regret darted through her heart.

This event had brought her to a shocking realization.

Why hadn't she spoken to him sooner about God? Why had she waited so long to bring him the words of life? Had she been awed by his position, his nobility?

Now, one promise from God's Book would give her comfort. This alone could give her hope: "My word . . . shall not return to Me void."

His young wife and his unborn child—surely in some way the light would come to these souls groping in sin and sorrow.

6 | The Silver Opium Box

That evening John and Olga gathered together the things they planned to take to camp. They placed trunks, suitcases, and beds on a cart that a coolie would drag to the Columbia Country Club where prisoners were to meet before being dispatched to the prison camp tomorrow. The beds they planned to drop off for safekeeping at the home of John Way.

As the evening wore on, friends—old and new—came to spend this last night of freedom with them. Somehow no one seemed sleepy. When the door opened to admit little Mrs. Lui, who had hobbled several blocks on her tiny bound feet to say good-bye to them, Olga had to choke back the tears. The unbreakable tie of Christianity bound them all together regardless of language barriers. She and John treasured the friendship of these people with whom they had mingled for many years.

A sudden commotion outside sent Olga running to the window. A coolie pulling a ricksha had stopped right at their door. The next minute one of the girls ushered in a woman, middle-aged and dressed in brocade and silks. Olga recognized her at once—Mrs. Laing, a relative of the famous Dr. Sun Yat-sen.

Now neither she nor John could hide their surprise. What was this woman—this daughter of nobility—doing here? Olga bubbled with pleasantry. "My dear Mrs. Laing, how nice to see you. But— how—why?" John stepped forward to greet her too.

"And why are you surprised, Mrs. Oss? Do you think I could let you, my dear friends, go away to an enemy camp without seeing you this night?" A lovely smile radiated from her pretty Oriental face. Just then the coolie came in carrying boxes. "We brought you some things you will need in camp—soap, toothpaste, sugar, cornstarch."

John, dependable as always, expressed their thanks and explained, "We will leave these things with friends who have promised to send packages each month as the Japanese will allow."

Olga suddenly found herself without words. She could only force a smile through her tears, but she felt grateful.

Mrs. Laing smiled her approval and glanced around the room. Noting the others who had gathered to spend the night there, she said, "I, too, have come to stay the night with you and John." While John hurried to make their latest guest comfortable, Olga for a moment felt herself far removed from the loyal and sympathetic group who filled the room. She was remembering. Time slipped back to the day she had first met this woman—this gem of aristocracy.

She saw herself one day hurrying down Tibet Road in the streets of Shanghai. The woman's clothes for one thing arrested Olga's attention—American style gray squirrel coat and muff plus other finery. And she was crying softly into a silk handkerchief. Olga found herself staring, though the woman seemed oblivious of everything.

An intuitive feeling came over Olga. This woman was in some kind of trouble. She stepped close and asked, "Madame, why are you crying? May I help you in some way?"

A pair of kind brown eyes glanced at her through soft tears. "No—no—no one can help me," came the hopeless words. It did not surprise Olga to hear her speak in perfect English. This woman was obviously educated and cultured.

"Perhaps if you will tell me why you are crying I *can* help you," persisted Olga.

The lady shook her head, leaving Olga with a helpless feeling. But she just couldn't walk away and leave this nice woman crying in the streets when the least she could do would be to say something that might comfort her.

"Where do you live?" Olga ventured.

"I have a room at the More Memorial," replied the despondent woman.

Olga nodded her head. She recognized the name of the Young Women's Christian Association, home for Christian workers.

"May I walk with you?" Olga asked.

The woman stopped crying and studied her. "All right, you may come to my room if you like."

Together they walked to the More Memorial Home and up to where the woman lived. Olga glanced around the room. Everything gave evidence that this woman was no pauper. But who was she?

Piled in a corner were several suitcases. A beautiful fur coat lay draped over a chair. In an open closet Olga spotted more fur coats. Lavish robes and dresses lay scattered about.

"Please sit down," invited the woman. "I really do not believe you can help me. I have a hopeless problem. In fact, I was just going out to rent a cheap hotel room and then I was going to take my life." She reached into her squirrel muff and pulled out a tiny silver box enameled exquisitely with hand-painted flowers. "I *want* to die." A sick sadness covered her countenance.

Olga recognized the little box instantly. It was the kind used by the wealthy Chinese to hold the best quality of high-grade opium. The poor used a cheaper grade of opium and did not keep it in silver boxes. She had witnessed, too, how the rich, pampered by special opium servants, indulged in the ritual of opium smoking.

The servant would break off a tiny bit of opium, twist the strand skillfully on a needle, hold it over an opium lamp, light it to just the right glow, then bring it to his master and place it in his opium pipe. The master would then smoke and float off into a world of delightful fantasy.

Olga was sure that the silver box contained the opium. She was convinced also that if one should swallow it in its raw state, swift and certain death would result.

Opening the box, the sad woman spoke with a determined tone, "I'm going to swallow this and die quickly."

Olga stepped forward and held out her hand, "Please give me that box. And please—won't you tell me why you want to take your life?" She mustered all the persuasive kindness her soul possessed.

The woman stared at her, yet did not move. "No—I *must* die. There is no other way."

Seeing her determination, Olga prayed, "Dear God, give me the right words to help this woman." She placed a hand on the woman's shoulder. "Please, before you take the opium, please—won't you tell me *why* you must die."

Silence. Then the poignant words: "All right, my husband has left me for another woman. I am valueless. There is nothing in life for me now—nothing." Fresh tears spilled onto the smooth face.

Disbelief first, then a rush of sympathy filled Olga's heart. How could her husband, whoever he was, leave this gentle, beautiful woman of refinement?

"You see," the grief-stricken lady whispered, "I could not bear him any children." The tragedy in her voice pierced Olga deeply. She could *feel* her torment. A barren woman in China was the worst kind of curse.

"Would you mind telling me your name?" Olga invited ever so gently.

"I am Mrs. Laing. I am related to the late Dr. Sun Yat-sen."

There was that name again.

Quietly Mrs. Laing continued her story while the tears spilled all over her cheeks. "My husband is a very wealthy man. But now —now I mean nothing to him." Fresh anguish convulsed her slender frame.

"Wait, Mrs. Laing," Olga held up her hands with appeal. "This life is not the end. Our God has promised us a new life in heaven. And if you take your own life, you will never go to heaven."

4—B.B.W.

Mrs. Laing looked up. As if to answer Olga's unspoken question, she said, "I am a Buddhist. You are a Christian, aren't you? I have always wondered about your God."

"Yes, I am a Christian. My husband and I have been in China for many years. We are missionaries. My name is Olga Oss. Mrs. Laing, as Christians, we believe that our God did not create us only to live and suffer and finally to die forever. He has a plan for us. He has promised a wonderful heaven if we believe in His plan. My dear, don't you see, this life is only a transition period in which to prepare for a better world?"

A little light crept into Mrs. Laing's eyes. "Please tell me more about your God." She spoke in a most gentle tone. The silver box slipped into her lap.

For the next two hours Olga reasoned with the woman, seeking to build a wall of faith against inflooding desperation. She presented as tactfully and sincerely as possible the God of Christianity and the hope of salvation. While Mrs. Laing listened with open interest she forgot to be sad.

At last Olga urged, "Now, Mrs. Laing, will you please give me that box?"

Again Mrs. Laing clutched the silver box. A faraway look came into her eyes. Then, relaxing her hold, she pleaded, "If I give it to you, Mrs. Oss, will you promise to become my friend and come to see me often?"

"Yes, of course I promise."

Mrs. Laing handed over the silver box. "You may keep this to remember me by." She managed a wan smile.

Olga slipped the box into her purse. Later she would dispose of the deadly opium.

"Now you cannot stay here by yourself, Mrs. Laing," Olga said to her new-found friend. "Where will you go from here? Let me help you to get settled."

"Dr. Lung and his wife have always been good friends of mine. I should like to stay with them," answered Mrs. Laing.

Again Olga recognized a name of prominence. Dr. Lung was the son of Dr. Sun Yat-sen.

Olga moved around the room. "All right. Let's get your things packed. I'll help you, and then I'll go with you." A grateful smile from Mrs. Laing convinced her anew that the Word of God is quick and powerful, and sharper than any two-edged sword.

In the days and months that followed, a strong friendship had developed between them. They spent many hours together searching the words of hope and life in the Bible. One day at last Mrs. Laing received Christ in baptism and became a fervent Seventh-day Adventist. Filled with new love for God and humanity, Mrs. Laing was touched to open her purse and make large contributions to church-operated hospitals in Shanghai.

Olga had to shake herself. How long had she been reminiscing? Now she was back in the little room, surrounded by wonderful friends and dear Mrs. Laing. This dear, gentle woman was ready to stand by the Osses this last night.

And not only that. She was to figure prominently in still another chapter of their wartime experiences later on. How John especially would have been heartened if he could have foreseen how God would use this friend, Mrs. Laing, as an instrument to save his life only a few short months away.

7 | Prisoners in a Japanese War Camp

The night passed quickly for the Osses, with everyone joining in singing hymns and offering prayers for their safety. When the first rays of the morning sun streaked the sky, a coolie brought Olga two corsages from friends. Though to wear them seemed to her a bit inappropriate, she decided to do so anyway.

Soon the procession started toward the place of rendezvous—the two missionaries, three coolies pushing and pulling the loaded cart, and a group of Chinese friends—a rather motley group plodding through the streets of Shanghai at that early hour. The friends insisted on accompanying the Osses all the way to the Columbia Country Club.

As the group approached the home of Mr. Way, John ordered the coolies to stop. They would unload their beds here for safekeeping until the day they were released. At the gate, a servant appeared and quickly and silently carried the beds into the house. Mr. Way came to the door and invited John and Olga to enter. But before they could accept his invitation they noticed a strange thing happening. The friends who had sung hymns, prayed, and stayed up all night with them, were now, one by one, edging away and leaving them, until they found themselves alone with just the coolies. And not one of them had said good-bye.

John and Olga stared at each other in silent amazement. What had happened? Why had their friends deserted them without explanation?

The answer came quickly. Out of nowhere, two men dressed in civilian clothing stepped forward and one slapped a coolie.

"We saw you take something inside that house. What are you

trying to hide? Speak, fool." Another slap sent the coolie reeling to the ground, leaving him speechless.

Olga's heart flipped a few times. Now she understood why their friends had quietly taken their leave. These men were Japanese spies!

The look on John's face showed that he too understood that these intruders who were now questioning them were Japanese spies. He stepped forward and spoke to them courteously. "We are on our way to the Columbia Country Club, as instructed by your consul."

"You are John and Olga Oss, are you not?"

"That is correct," replied John.

The man's attitude seemed to change and now he spoke politely. "You will continue quickly to the country club. Buses will be there to take you to camp." The two men turned and walked away. Olga heaved a sigh of relief.

John Way, who had witnessed the scene with disgust, said, "I am so sorry. Is there anything more that I can do for you?" He seemed so anxious to help.

"No," Olga replied. "And how is Mrs. Way today?"

His face saddened. "She is at very low ebb."

Impulsively, Olga asked, "Do you mind if we have a short prayer before we go?"

John Way, by now not entirely unfamiliar with the ways of Christianity, nodded. "Yes, please do."

The three knelt and John offered a brief prayer asking God to be with each one of them in the trying days ahead and reunite them one day in friendship, if it be His will. Then, afraid they were still being watched, they extended their hands to say good-bye. John Way gripped each hand tightly and bowed. Again they were on their way, following the coolies pulling the cart.

Arriving at the Columbia Country Club, they soon found themselves lost among the hundreds of Americans, Britishers, Netherlanders, Belgians, and white Russians, all destined for the same prison camp. The majority, however, appeared to be Americans.

Everywhere was confusion. Japanese workers tossed luggage hit and miss in every direction. John and Olga found themselves dodging to avoid being hit. Looking around, they saw some strange sights. There were women—destined for prison camp—dressed in the formal evening clothes they had worn the night before at farewell parties. Some wore low-cut gowns. It soon became evident that a number had spent their last free night in drunken revelry.

Men and women still reeled in drunken stupor, laughing and talking foolishly. A woman sitting in a corner on her suitcase cried and wrung her hands. Standing together, apart from the others, were a group of thirteen nuns and several Catholic priests. The international congregation included a wide number of business executives, airline and steamship officials, many missionaries, and not a few tourists who had been caught in the web of war.

All moved about with nervous excitement. In the midst of the hubbub a woman, without aplomb, dressed in a low-cut black shimmering gown, came up to Olga and blurted out in thick accent, "Say, dearie, where do you think you're going—on a trip around the world?" Laughing loudly, she reeled back and forth on spike heels. Reaching out, she fingered the two corsages which Olga wore on her hand-knit blue suit.

Olga looked around with embarrassment. Others seemed to be staring at her too. Question marks on the faces of some even indicated they were questioning her mentality! But she couldn't see anything wrong with wearing the lovely orchids and roses—tokens of their friends' devotion. Perhaps it would be a long time before she would see or smell flowers again. Let them stare. She wouldn't take them off.

Seeing a woman seated on her suitcase and crying into her hands, Olga stepped in her direction. The young woman, dressed in a flimsy gown, shuddered and shivered. Olga removed her own scarf and placed it around the lady's shoulders. A pair of tear-stained eyes looked up gratefully, but no words seemed to come.

Then she noticed the flowers and smiled. But her expression said, "Oh, no, lady, you can't be serious, wearing two corsages at a time like this!" Olga patted her shoulder and walked away.

Loud sobs could be heard everywhere in the lobby, since few seemed to attempt hiding their worried feelings. As for Olga, she could not shed a tear. And she wasn't afraid anymore. God had taken away her fear, and she was determined to keep an outward expression of her faith without crying or complaining. After all, she and John were together, and for the time being this was all that mattered.

Then Satan whispered, "If you hadn't come to China as missionaries you would be safely home now in the States."

But fresh in her mind were the words of languid Mrs. Way, hovering in the valley of death. Her voice rang clear yet. "Because you came to China, Mrs. Oss, I have learned to know your God." No one could take away the joy of those words. No matter what happened, she could never be sorry they had come to China as missionaries. God would see them through. With this she turned her back on the evil one.

The cries of a girl about fourteen years of age suddenly caught her attention. The girl clung to her parents in terror. It was apparent that the girl was going to the prison camp and her parents were not. Leaving John again, she walked up and addressed the girl. "Is there something I can do to help?" The distraught girl continued to sob and cling to her parents.

The mother looked into Olga's face, and spoke with distress. "We have a problem. Our daughter is now a prisoner of the Japanese, and we are not. You see, she was born on an American ship and was permitted to claim American citizenship. We are not American citizens." She nodded toward her husband.

At once Olga saw the problem. "My name is Olga Oss," she began. "My husband and I are Americans and have spent many years in China as missionaries. Perhaps I can do something to help your child in camp."

Tears of gratitude streamed down the mother's face. "Oh, you are missionaries?"

"Yes, of the Seventh-day Adventist Church."

"Well, Mrs. Oss, we would ask that you take our child, Anna, under your wing and give her a guiding hand. Please, would you do us this favor? We will remember you for your kindness. She is so young."

Olga could not suppress the sympathy she felt for this family, particularly for the young girl about to be separated from her parents. Without hesitation she replied, "Of course, I shall do all I can to help her and guide her. Please do not worry." She held out a hand for the girl.

Time was running short. The girl's parents promised to keep in touch with them. A loud stir and bustle among the people indicated that buses had arrived. Soon they would be on their way to prison camp. Suddenly there was a loud crescendo of nervous good-byes. A Japanese soldier, fully armed, called. "Time to board buses. Board buses."

The parents tore themselves away from their child, and Olga led her by the hand back to John who was waiting for her. "I'll explain later," she told him when he eyed the girl.

One by one, men, women, and children, some very young, some old, were shoved into the undersized buses. John held Olga's hand tightly, and she in turn kept the bewildered girl close to her. As more and more jammed into the buses, the odor of bodies and alcohol mingled to permeate the limited space. Arms, legs, elbows jostled in every direction, until all were settled like sardines in a can.

The bus's engine gave a sudden roar, and they were off. Squeezing John's hand, Olga asked, "Where do you think the camp is? Where do you think they'll take us?"

John's eyes said, "Don't fret, darling; we're still together, aren't we?"

The wheels of the bus rolled over the streets of Shanghai, past the mission compound where they had lived, then across a railroad track and by St. John's University. They had traveled only a few miles when the bus slowed down. Suddenly it came to a bumpy halt. John stretched his neck to look. "Why, this is the Great China University. We're only five miles from downtown Shanghai. We're on the northwestern edge of the city." His face brightened with a pleased look.

"Wasn't this bombed by the Japanese when the war started?" Olga wanted to know.

"Yes, it certainly was. But it looks as if there are still a few buildings standing," John observed.

The bus door opened and a soldier stepped into the bus. "This is the Chapei Civilian Assembly Center. You will go to the building on the left," he commanded. "The building in the center is a Japanese chemical plant. If Americans bomb this place, you will all be killed." He laughed as he said this, evidently enjoying the thought.

The luggage had followed them on trucks, and now the soldiers were tossing and kicking suitcases and other items like footballs, in all directions.

John and Olga and the girl followed the others through two large entrance gates. "Look, John," Olga cried. "Look at that double row of thick barbed wire." The twelve-acre campus was encompassed by two rows of barbed wire, eight feet high and fifteen feet apart, the space between making a path around the camp. Sixteen guards armed with guns and bayonets were already patrolling the area.

It was evident that the damage caused by the bombing had been hastily repaired, although devastation and piles of rubble remained on all sides. Windows had been blown out of the remaining two large buildings. These edifices, known as the East and West Buildings, would house the prisoners. Off to one side in the center was the chemical plant which the soldier had pointed out. An electrified fence surrounded it.

In the center of the campus grew several tall ginkgo trees, leaves shining in the crisp February sun. Olga noticed the groves of willow trees that dotted the campus, and her heart felt a joyous lift. At least there were trees in this prison camp. And around the outer edge of the campus a stream flowed, making a pleasant scene.

The guards, who were Japanese consular police under a commandant, directed them. "You will go to room 15, East Building." And to the now silent young girl he commanded, "You will go to room 39." Olga was glad. At least they would be in the same building. Olga smiled at the girl, nodding her head with encouragement. The girl obeyed.

The Osses made their way to the assigned room, and discovered that it was a classroom about 34 x 15 feet. Before long the eleven people who would occupy it had arrived. After the beds were set up, only a few inches of corridor space remained between them. And it turned out that every occupant was a missionary. There were Methodist, Presbyterian, Episcopalian, Christian Alliance, Assemblies of God, and Seventh-day Adventist missionaries, the Osses being the Adventists.

When Olga and John saw the sturdy, roomy beds that others had brought, they regretted that they had left their good beds with John Way and taken along only light cots. Others had used better judgment, they reflected. Because some had already set up their beds, John had to place his cot against the wall and Olga's across from his, with a door between that would swing every time someone used it. The room had three bombed-out windows and a door on either side. Some with more foresight than Olga and John, placed their beds under the windows for fresh air. They too loved fresh air, but had unthinkingly occupied space away from the windows.

As the hours wore away and evening came on, John exclaimed, "I'm getting hungry. I wonder where we eat." To which a fellow-missionary answered, "Oh, haven't you heard? Because of all the commotion in getting settled, there won't be any supper tonight.

Nothing until tomorrow morning. Don't you have a candy bar or something?"

John remembered that they did have a few candy bars in their suitcases. This then would be their meal, their first in camp.

As the hour grew late, the excitement that had followed them to camp was replaced by a strange silence. All seemed exhausted, confused, and worried. Olga, looking around the room, was struck by a sudden realization. "John, how can we undress in this room, with all these people?" Her voice, though a whisper, was obviously heard by others in the room, all being in such close proximity.

Wearily, John glanced around the room, then at his wife. She studied his face as he, too, wrestled with the problem that faced all eleven of them. What would they do for privacy?

8 | Early Days at Camp

While Olga sat on her narrow cot and wondered what to do next, others were attempting to hang sheets, tableclothes, and even towels for dividers. The difficulty was that no matter how much they tried to avoid it, they found themselves infringing on each other's few feet of floor space. For the present, however, no one seemed to object, so John proceeded to hang up a sheet which Olga had taken from their suitcase under the cot. The room was now draped with waving banners of all colors, sizes, and patterns, providing a semblance of privacy, however little.

As all readied for bed, Olga's cot, behind the door, received a bang whenever anyone went in or out. John's cot ended up foot to foot with Josephine Marie's, the young daughter of the Christian Alliance missionary. Two tiny electric lights provided a dim light for the room. Somehow Olga managed to get into her nightclothes and fell exhausted onto her cot. A lingering fragrance from the treasured flowers brought her a little comfort. John came over and whispered, "Good night, darling." He smiled and kissed her gently, and both settled down for their first night in camp.

Olga's bed was foot to foot with Mr. Krug's. When this gentleman deposited his six-foot body and two hundred pounds of weight on his light cot, Olga held her breath. But the cot only creaked loudly, causing everyone to turn and see if he had fallen through.

Many moments of confusion passed as various ones prepared for bed behind their improvised partitions. At nine o'clock, without warning, the lights went out. In the dark, from all around the room, came the thud of shoes dropping to the floor, and the sound of belts being unbuckled or of clothes being unsnapped or unzipped. Olga's thoughts raced around in circles. This room held people from all parts of the globe. What were their thoughts? How would each adjust to this new life? How long would they live crowded in this manner? Offering a prayer for all of them, she closed her eyes and tried to sleep.

Suddenly Mr. Krug was praying. Out loud. "Heavenly Father, some have already taken more than their share of this room. Teach them, O Lord, that unselfishness is a divine virtue." On and on he offered his fervent petitions on his knees, until at last his room-mates heard the loud, grinding cre-ee-eak of his cot. Then all was still.

Moments later, his puffs, wheezes, and snores filled the room. Olga wondered how she would ever get used to this human saw-mill so near her—so near in fact that his big feet overlapped onto her cot. She was still trying to fall asleep when loud noises came from across the hall. A man's discordant voice was singing, "Show me the way to go home." It dawned on her at once that the man was drunk. Hoping that the guards on the second floor would not hear, she was grateful that their room was full of missionaries. They at least would not have drunkenness to contend with.

Hardly had she closed her eyes again when a woman's voice called loudly in the darkness. "Does anyone know where the cubicle is?" Hearing John stir in his cot, she whispered, "Does she have to yell?"

John replied quietly, "She is deaf, dear. Her husband told me."

Again Mrs. Adams called, louder this time. "Does anyone know where the cubicle is?"

A voice in the dark wanted to know, "What does she mean, cubicle? These Britishers!"

In reply to Mrs. Adams's question someone called, "The bath-room is down the hall."

Mrs. Adams was right. It was a cubicle, nothing more. Just a few square feet of space. And every time the flush chain was pulled, the water tank hanging from the ceiling poured water onto the floor. So the floor was always flooded. Olga hoped Mrs. Adams wouldn't get herself drowned.

She was about to drift off to sleep again after a quiet spell when she heard the voice of old and deaf Mrs. Adams again. "Where's my pottie?" she was asking. Chuckles rippled around the room. A thump and a clang finally indicated that Mrs. Adams had located the missing fixture. Olga had to smile to herself. Once again she pulled the covers up over her shoulders. The room was unheated, and it was difficult to keep warm.

The banging of the door against her bed awakened her early the next morning. Guards were hurrying up and down the hall, speaking in perfect English, "Line up for roll call in the hallway." Fumbling around, she managed somehow to dress under the covers. Would she ever get used to this lack of privacy? she wondered.

John was already up and dressed. "Good morning, dear," he greeted her. "How did you sleep?" Looking calm and cheerful, he smiled as though they were not at all in a prison camp. What a pillar of faith her John was!

"Oh, I slept well, once I fell asleep." But she could not help smiling again at the humorous interruptions that had kept her awake a long time. They walked together into the drafty hallway, joining the others who had lined up quietly.

A guard shouted, "The commandant is arriving. You will all bow."

The commandant strutted down the hall followed by several guards. Dressed in full uniform, he sported a long, curved samurai sword, and a big pistol hung from his side. One of the guards stepped forward and placed a small table in the center of the hallway. The commandant clicked his heels and halted. The company of prisoners bowed in unison. Olga felt her heart galloping. What would this officer say to them?

Without a word, the commandant, about five feet in height, stepped onto the table. Now he could look down on all his prisoners, some of whom were six feet and over.

As he spoke, he revealed a large set of beautiful white teeth. "You are prisoners of warrr—." He savored the words and paused, "This camp is called Chapei Civilian Assembly Center, by order of the Japanese government. You will NOT call this a prison camp!" His slight body was as straight as a board. He paused again to note the impact of his words.

Silently Olga reacted. "Why shouldn't this be called an internment camp? Aren't we prisoners of war?" As if in answer to her question, the commandant shouted into the air.

"No harm will come to you as long as the American Government does no harm to our Japanese people in American prison camps. If they do, we will KILL all of you." The words came in perfect English. "And," he continued, "should any of you attempt to run away you will be shot. Remember, you are heavily guarded." Olga recalled that she had counted sixteen guards between the two rows of heavy barbed wire.

"The operation and maintenance of this camp will be your responsibility. You will grow your own vegetables, do your own cooking, wash your own clothing, and provide for your own general care. You will organize and distribute duties among yourselves. And remember, anyone who tries to escape will be shot." Turning to his assistant, he ordered, "Number off."

Roll call began. One—two—three—until each person represented by a number had been accounted for.

It was noted that among the group of prisoners—and they were prisoners in spite of euphemisms—there were several Japanese-Americans. Were they real Americans, or were they spies? Regardless, they were eyed with suspicion by the others. The small commandant stepped off the table and walked briskly out of the hallway, followed by his guards.

A line formed in the kitchen where breakfast was being served. One man in line asked Olga, "What's for breakfast? Bacon and eggs?" Obviously, he was joking.

Glancing at the passing plates, Olga replied, "It looks like oat-

meal." Since they had been instructed to take along their own eating utensils, she and John had brought aluminum pie plates. Now
she wished they had brought bowls.

A scoop of oatmeal and a cup of cocoa, and that was breakfast.
They carried the food to their room and sat on their beds. Later
there would be an eating area for them, they were told. The oatmeal was thin, and Olga asked John, "What are these little chunks
in the oatmeal?"

"Looks like raisins," he replied, taking a mouthful. "Nice to
have raisins in our cereal."

After breakfast came the work of organization. Mr. Black, the
Episcopalian missionary, was assigned to be room monitor for their
room. Mr. Drew, an airline executive with a knack for organiz-
ing, was chosen as one of the camp superintendents. Olga volunteered that she had had experience in dietetics and was assigned
to the kitchen. John went to work with others in the vegetable
garden.

A few days later, Olga made a discovery in the kitchen. The
sacks of oatmeal stacked in a corner carried a FRANCE label. She
wondered how they had ever made their way to this part of the
world. Opening one of the sacks, she noticed that the oatmeal
heaved in a strange manner. She fingered a handful of the moving
cereal, and raised it to her nostrils. Dropping it, she gasped, "Why,
this oatmeal is full of *worms*. So these are the raisins in the cereal!"
How could she and John, or *anyone,* ever eat another mouthful
of this stuff? Why, the sack heaved with vermin. Then she remembered that John had already lost weight, and so had she. But
she had better not say a word. Oatmeal with worms was better
than starving to death.

Shortly after Olga's oatmeal discoverey, a young American—a
stranger to her—sauntered into the kitchen looking for some
breakfast. Introducing himself as a newcomer, he said, "I worked
for the Kalan Mining Co., but now here I am. Where can I get
some food?"

"Right here, young man." Olga smiled at the eager and hungry fellow, who could not suspect what awaited him in the cereal. Dipping a ladle into the oatmeal pot, she poured it into his bowl. After the first mouthful, the young man picked out the "raisins" and set them to one side. Soon he had more "raisins" than oatmeal.

"What's the matter?" Olga asked.

"What are these things that look like raisins?" he held one between his fingers.

How she hated to tell him. Reluctantly, she said, "I am sorry, young man, but they are worms." Blunt as it sounded, he had a right to know.

The young fellow dropped his mouth, his eyes filled with incredulity. "Do you mean we are supposed to *eat* them?"

"Yes, young man. We eat them, or else go terribly hungry. There is no choice." Olga shook her head.

He stared, but only for a few seconds. His next move surprised her. Scooping the "raisins" into his spoon, he raised them in midair. "Guess I'd better eat them too. Can't starve." And he swallowed them in one gulp.

Olga found herself patting the courageous young man's shoulder.

As the work of organization continued, a list was compiled, containing the names of all ordained ministers of every denomination. When the list was distributed, the name of John Oss, who was an ordained minister for the Seventh-day Adventist Church, did not appear. As the days passed John was given no recognition. Although each minister in his room took turns in offering prayer and preparing religious services, John was not asked to participate. Together he and Olga prayed that somehow the apparent prejudice would melt away.

On the campus near the entrance gate, not far from the barbed wire, stood a three-sided shelter, formerly used as a bus stop. This served as the camp's chapel, where both Protestants and Catholics worshiped, a few boards having been framed together to make an altar. Although ignored by the other missionaries, John continued to do all in his power to be cooperative, working hours beyond the call of duty, and treating everyone with extreme kindness.

One day Mr. Black, the room monitor, called John for an unpleasant assignment. After the passing of several weeks, it was obvious that Mr. Krug had not yet learned that his supplications before retirement had best be offered in silence. Night after night he continued to bring before God, loud and clear, the problems that beset him during the day. When he prayed, "Heavenly Father, today several of our missionary brethren sneaked away to connive in secret meeting. But, Lord, condemn them not, for there is no light in the doctrines taught in their churches," tempers till then held in restraint broke loose with fiery indignation. They elected John to speak to him about his offensive habit.

Unpleasant as this assignment was, John did not shirk. Calling Mr. Krug apart, he appealed to him quietly. "Brother Krug, you live close to the Lord, and we are happy that you are a praying man. But there are some in our room, who, though they do not wish to reveal the fact, are not well physically. Talking of any kind during the night disturbs their rest. For their sakes, Brother Krug, would you pray silently to our heavenly Father?"

Brother Krug appeared surprised, yet responded to John's tactful appeal. He agreed to stop his public prayers.

It was not long after they had arrived in camp that Olga was reading the *North China Daily News,* which thus far was permitted in camp. Remembering the words of John Way, she scanned the obituary column each day for news of Mrs. Way, whom she had left at death's door.

Now here it appeared: "Died, beloved wife of John Way. . . ." At the very end of the obituary were the words—the message Mr. Way had promised to convey—"I will fear no evil: for Thou art with me."

The words pierced her heart. Turning to John, she cried, "Here it is, John, the message John Way promised to send—words from the twenty-third psalm. Imagine, a Buddhist quoting these words from the Bible. If we ever get out of here, we must keep in touch with him." She brushed the tears from her eyes.

John shared her sadness and the happiness she felt in knowing that the words of the psalmist could bring peace and comfort even to non-Christians.

The weeks lengthened into months, and the sticky heat of summer came with a plague of countless mosquitoes. The food, at first, had been tolerable. The Red Cross had supplied powdered milk, cocoa, and good rice. But as these supplies dwindled and none came to replenish them, the food problem assumed critical proportions. The Japanese supplied them with coarse vegetables to supplement what they managed to grow in their garden, mostly turnips and Chinese cabbage. Also substandard grades of fish and meat, hard brown bread, and an inferior grade of rice. Eventually, salt, oil, and sugar vanished, and meat was seldom seen. Without seasonings of any kind, dishes became unpalatable, and many prisoners showed signs of losing weight.

International law stated that prisoners of war were to receive at least 1,200 calories of food per day. But as the days crept by, rations became even shorter. Everyone complained of hunger. The large stomachs that some had carried now vanished. Trousers began to hang loose. Since there were no facilities for sewing and repairing, some used rope, pins, nails, or anything at all that would take up the slack. The women, with less of a problem, simply allowed their dresses to hang loosely from their shoulders.

Friends of the Osses had kept their promise to send them monthly packages of supplies during their early stay. These came through the Swiss government. Now these had stopped coming. Even necessary items, such as soap and toothpaste, were unobtainable. One bar of soap provided by the Japanese each month for each prisoner was to be used for bathing and laundry.

When the camp superintendent announced early one morning that that evening there would be feasting on roast pork, a wave of excitement and gastronomic anticipation swept through the camp. Tonight there would be a feast.

A large truck pulled up before the camp kitchen, and the carcass of a whole pig was tossed onto the kitchen floor. Only the entrails had been removed. Mr. Drew, on hand for the occasion, along with others, decided to inspect the meat before they cooked it. Olga, on duty in the kitchen, came close.

As they bent over the carcass, they were swept back by a putrifying smell. "This pig looks like it has been dragged in the mud all the way from Shanghai!" Mr. Drew recoiled with anger. "It stinks!"

"Yes, it does smell bad," Olga agreed.

Looking closer, they saw maggots crawling over the pork. Olga gasped with horror and backed away. Mr. Drew's face grew red. "It's rotten, absolutely rotten!" He held his nose.

"What shall we do with it?" Olga wanted to know.

Mr. Drew snarled, "We'll throw it away, that's what we'll do." He called a helper, and the two of them dragged the carcass out of the kitchen all the way out to the row of barbed-wire fences. The armed guard was patrolling the area.

"When I say 'ready' we'll toss it over the fence," he directed. "OK, ready." The unwanted porker went flying over the fence and landed right in the path of the oncoming guard.

Instantly the guard reached for his gun and aimed.

"Dear God, don't let him shoot them," Olga prayed. The guard's eyes zigzagged in every direction. Sensing (and smelling) the motive behind the prisoners' act, he stayed his hand and hurried to inform the commandant.

But the commandant made no allowance for squeamish weakness. Like wildfire his order swept through the camp. Every prisoner was to line up before him. One by one they came from every direction. Some wore expressions of bewilderment. There had been no time to explain to many what had happened.

When all the prisoners were standing quietly before the commandant, he clicked his heels and stepped onto the table shouting, "YOU HAVE THROWN *FOOD*—A LARGE PIG—OVER THE FENCE." Eyes smoldering and face discolored with rage, the little man fingered his gun.

Shocked—horrified—men, women, and children stood helpless. What would this little man do to them?

"You will regret your fool's act today," barked the angry commandant. "There will be no meat, of any kind, served in this camp until further notice." He turned and left.

True to his word, he saw to it that no meat was provided for several weeks. Although John and Olga were unaffected, many felt the blow keenly. Now every morsel of food became precious.

9 | Please, Commandant, Just a Week's Honeymoon

Olga was directing activities in the kitchen one morning, when she heard Tom Barry's familiar voice. "Mrs. Oss, may I speak with you in private?" She turned and faced the tall, fine-featured redhead, a wealthy airline executive before his camp days. Now he helped most willingly in the kitchen.

"Of course, Tom." Olga smiled and put down a large stirring spoon.

"Mrs. Oss, I—I—that is—Hanna and me—we want to get married."

For a few seconds Olga just looked at the young man, who might just as well have casually announced, "Olga, the war has ended." That statement would have seemed almost as incredible.

Yet, Olga mused, why should she be surprised at all? Hadn't everyone noticed how much time he and the blue-eyed Dutch girl were spending together lately? Even the guards must have noticed. As scullery maid, Hanna had been conveniently able to perform her duties near Tom.

Regaining her composure, Olga answered, "Tom, you really want to get married *here* in this Japanese prison camp?"

Tom's unswerving reply was, "Yes, ma'am, right here in camp."

"But the commandant certainly would not permit it. And if he did, where would you get married? Where would you honeymoon? Where would you live?"

"Mrs. Oss, we've been secretly engaged for months," Tom confided, as though this made the whole thing more sensible.

Somehow Olga couldn't keep the warm glow out of her voice. "I've guessed you two were in love."

64

Tom's blue eyes sparked with encouragement. "Mrs. Oss, do you think—do you suppose—*you* could go to the commandant and ask for permission for us to get married? I'm sure our priest, Father Carrs, would marry us."

Olga stepped back. "Me?" She smiled with unbelief. "My dear young man, why me?"

"Well, because you're a missionary. Maybe he will feel more kindly toward you if you ask, instead of me."

The pleading look in the young man's eyes touched Olga's heart. She found herself saying, "All right, Tom. If you feel that way about it, I'll go and ask him tomorrow morning, but don't set your heart on it."

Tom Barry gave Olga a bear hug. "Thanks, Mrs. Oss, you're just great." Somehow he seemed so confident that she would be successful. She wished she could share some of his confidence.

It didn't take long for the word to get around that Tom and Hanna were going to ask the commandant for permission to be married in the prison camp.

"Are they crazy?" some asked.

"And what would they use for a church? Not that bus-stop shed they call a chapel!" others added.

"Maybe the commandant will let them honeymoon in Tokyo," joked another.

Hearing all these remarks, Olga reasoned that the whole idea did seem a little ludicrous. But since she had committed herself to Tom, she would make the appeal to the commandant. Who knew? He was a human being. Once he too had doubtless been in love. He was married, wasn't he? And the rumor was that he had an American wife, now back in her own country.

When she told John what she was planning to do, John smiled and said, "Really, Olga, you do walk where angels fear to tread." Reaching for her hand, he encouraged, "But go ahead, help cupid along."

The next morning after Olga had brushed her long golden hair and dressed as neatly as possible, she ventured toward the commandant's office. The guard standing with gun and fixed bayonet at the door eyed her closely. Coming nearer, Olga explained, "I've come to speak with the commandant. May I go in?"

The guard clicked his heels and turned. "I go see."

Somehow, now, Olga found herself taking deep breaths. Did she have the nerve? What would she actually say to this big boss? How could she tell him that human emotions had not died completely here in this miserable prison camp, and that even if there was a war raging outside, love still found a way? Would he hear her out, or ask her to leave immediately?

Oh, well, there was no turning back now. Here goes!

The returning guard snapped, "You may go in."

The small commandant sat behind a huge desk. Seeing Olga he raised only his eyeballs. Olga stood before his desk and bowed low —very low. No greeting came from the commandant. She straightened and forced the words that seemed stuck in her throat, "Commandant Tursuki, I have come to make a very special request."

The commandant's eyes narrowed. "What is it this time?" The American-educated chief spoke perfect English.

"Well, you see, we have two young people in camp—one a Dutch girl from Singapore—" Olga stopped. Really now, which words would she choose to express the idea of falling in love? The commandant glared and waited.

Glancing at his cold eyes, Olga wondered. Did he have a heart? Had he ever been in love? At this moment, neither seemed possible.

"Go on," commanded the little man.

"All right," the words tumbled out. "These two young people have fallen in love!" Now that it was out she was beginning to feel terribly foolish. This man—why should he care? Didn't he desire their very lives? Wouldn't he take them if he dared? If it would not jeopardize the lives of his Japanese countrymen in America?

The commandant raised his head and stared as if he could not believe this woman was standing before him. "And what is this very special request?" He seemed curious now.

"Sir, they would like your permission to get married."

No reply came. The commandant only stared. Could he hear her thumping heart? Was he completely stunned?

"Married?"

Olga nodded. Perhaps she should turn and leave now.

"So they want to be married?" Suddenly a strange smile came to his face. "You know, Mrs. Oss, if they were fools enough to fall in love—why, why yes, they may be married."

The waves of joy and relief that rolled over Olga almost keeled her over. Outwardly she brightened and smiled. Speaking quickly lest he change his mind, she said, "Oh, thank you, sir. They will need official papers through your office. We can arrange for Father Carrs to perform the wedding. We'll let you know the date."

Taking her leave, she bowed lower than ever. Thank God, thank God, beneath that austere uniform this officer had a heart.

Tom and Hanna came running to meet her. Olga's smiles gave the good news away. "You are two lucky people," she said.

"Tell us, tell us quick, Mrs. Oss, what did he say?" Tom pressed.

"You can thank the good Lord that that man has a heart beneath that uniform of war. He actually gave permission for you two to get married."

Tom and Hanna jumped all around the kitchen embracing each other.

"We'll have a real wedding," Tom promised Hanna.

"Yes, we'll invite our friends and everyone who wants to attend," beamed Hanna.

"Well, there are a few problems to solve first," observed Olga. "Will you settle for the open-air chapel to be married in?"

Tom and Hanna looked at each other. Why not?

Olga foresaw many problems before the young couple and, wanting to help, offered to see about baking a wedding cake and finding a wedding dress for Hanna to wear.

"But, Mrs. Oss, where can we get the ingredients to make the wedding cake?" Hanna wanted to know. Flour, sugar, and other supplies had long since disappeared from the prison larder. Cakes and sweets were only delicacies to be dreamed of.

"Just leave that part to me," Olga said. "And give me a list of the guests you will invite to the wedding. By the way, have you set the date?"

"One week from today," Tom said. "I wonder what I'll do for a wedding ring." A solution seemed to cross his mind and he remained silent.

During the few days remaining before the wedding, Olga worked with high spirits to prepare the bride for the ceremony. What would they use for a wedding dress? Remembering that some of the women had worn formal dresses the first evening in camp, Olga decided to scout around for a white one if possible. Rapping at every door, she found one lady finally who was willing to loan a beautiful white satin gown which she had foolishly worn to camp. Another lady offered her white high-heeled shoes.

Olga found an old dirty torn piece of mosquito net in the kitchen which belonged to no one. This she washed. Holding up the flimsy piece of material, she said to the prospective bridegroom, "Tom, I have a needle and some white thread. If you can find me a piece of wire, I'll patch this mosquito net and shirr it for a veil for Hanna."

Soon the mosquito net was transformed into a dainty bridal veil.

Next, ingredients for the wedding cake. Checking names on Hanna's wedding-guest list, Olga started scouting again. Since packages had stopped coming from the Red Cross, all those who could had hoarded supplies, and Olga knew that a few might still have some precious flour, powdered milk, and sugar. She found enough who would contribute a few tablespoons of wormy flour. Others gave small amounts of powdered milk. None would give precious sugar. One lady having a few Chinese dates offered these to Olga for sweetening the cake.

Tom improvised a brick oven in which to bake the wedding cake. First Olga soaked the hard dates. Next she sifted the wormy flour, added the rest of the meager ingredients, and poured the unusual-looking batter into the largest flat kitchen pan. While baking, the cake managed to rise a little; and when Olga removed it from the oven she was pleased with its appearance. "Too bad we don't have anything to use for icing," she said.

Olga sent Tom down by the creek to pick some sprigs of mint leaves. These would do to make some mint tea to serve with the cake, even though it would be sugarless.

The morning of the wedding dawned pleasant. Olga helped to dress the glowing bride. While the white gown hung loosely on the slender bride and the shoes were a size too big, no bride ever radiated more joy. Olga gave a last-minute touch to her beautiful blond hair, and soon the bridal party made its way to the open-air chapel, where all the wedding guests had gathered and the excited groom waited.

Father Carrs, dressed in priestly robes, performed the Catholic ceremony. Tom and Hanna knelt before him. After the final words, "I pronounce you man and wife," Tom reached into his pocket for the ring and placed it—a nail fashioned into a circle—on the bride's slender finger. Beads of perspiration dotted his forehead. As everyone watched, suddenly Tom slumped forward in a dead faint. The bride knelt before her husband calling, "Tom, Tom, what is wrong? Speak to me."

It took only a few seconds to revive the bridegroom and help him and his bride to the kitchen for refreshments. Every wedding guest had brought his own dish and cup and now held them out to receive the one-inch piece of wedding cake and sugarless tea.

Olga pulled John aside and whispered, "John, they have to have a honeymoon, don't they?"

John looked as though the thought had never occurred to him. "Why, that's right, they do. Now, Olga, what do you have in mind?"

Olga smiled. "I have an idea. Let me talk to Tom first." Olga motioned the groom to her side. "Tom," her voice was a bare whisper, "how would you like to have a honeymoon? I'm quite willing to go and ask the commandant."

Tom could not hide his joy. "Will you, will you, Mrs. Oss? Will you really? Do you think he would?"

"Well, I'll try." Tom squeezed her hand.

Sneaking away from the wedding group, Olga found herself once more before the commandant. Again she bowed very low. Again she received the commandant's glare. What was he thinking of her this time?

"Commandant," began Olga, "in America there is a custom. When a couple gets married they usually go away on a honeymoon."

Amazement sprung the commandant's mouth wide open, but he couldn't utter a word.

"Well, there are sixty people in the same room with Tom Barry and his bride. It would be very wonderful if you could let them go out for a honeymoon." Olga stopped to take a deep breath.

The commandant rose to his full five feet and managed finally to find his voice. "What do you think this is, a playhouse?" he shouted. "That's the trouble with you Americans! Don't you know that this is WAR? The answer is NO!"

Olga couldn't give up now. "But, sir, where will they go now that they are married?"

"That is not my problem!"

Olga felt a wild racing through her brain. Suddenly she remembered something—the crazy room. Right now it was empty. The Japanese never allowed anyone who suffered from mental depression to remain there long. They immediately transferred them to the prison hospital in Shanghai, for fear they would have to answer to the powers that be for producing insanity in the prison camp.

"Well, sir, there's no one in the isolation [she didn't dare say "crazy"} room right now. Would you allow them to have that room for their honeymoon?"

Livid with incredulity, the commandant barked "No!"

"Please, sir, couldn't they just have it for a month?"

This time the commandant snorted with laughter. Olga couldn't believe it. "No!" He rocked back and forth.

"Can they have it for three weeks?"

"No!" he shouted, still laughing.

"Can they have it for two weeks?"

"No!"

"Well, sir, can they have it for one week?"

The commandant stopped laughing and stared at the woman who had the audacity that only a stupid American would have.

"Yes," came the shocking reply.

10 | John Oss Leaves Camp

One day the internees voted to make changes in the camp's organization. This time Olga, receiving all but seven votes, was put in charge of women's and children's affairs. John was voted in as room monitor, and by Thanksgiving Day his name had also been placed on the roster of ministers who took turns officiating at church services. That John should now be recognized as a minister of God brought them much happiness.

Hardly had Olga assumed her new duties when a Mr. Huss asked her, "Are you Russian?"

Much surprised, Olga replied, "No, but my name is Russian. My mother named me after the grand duchess of Russia. I am an American."

"Where did you work before coming here?"

"At the Shanghai Clinic and Hospital on Range Road."

"You mean the new one?"

"Yes."

Mr. Huss's face was now a wreath of smiles.

"I am very well acquainted with Dr. Butka at the hospital. In fact, Dr. Butka examined me when I was very ill last year. He told me I'd have to have surgery. Well, I told him that I couldn't afford surgery, and I guessed I'd have to die. Do you know what he said?"

Olga could guess but did not want to say anything. She shook her head. Mr. Huss continued:

"The doctor said, 'Anyone can have surgery in this hospital!'

" 'How much will it cost?' I inquired.

" 'Twenty coppers,' [three or four cents] the doctor said.

" 'Do you really mean that, doctor?' I asked.

" 'Of course,' he replied."

Still smiling broadly, Mr. Huss continued, "I want to tell you something, Mrs. Oss. I didn't want to vote for you because I thought you were Russian. I even influenced others not to vote for you. But if you belong to the Shanghai Clinic, we'll work with you. Come to me if you have any trouble with anyone."

True to his word, Mr. Huss and many others became Olga's backbone in camp while she went about her duties.

One morning a great deal of activity seemed to be going on in the room across the hall. A steady stream of traffic came and went. Deciding that it was her job to investigate, Olga stepped into the hall and, seeing the door open, walked into the room.

Her eyes scanned at once a large blackboard with squares, and on it figures constantly being changed by the man in charge.

"Well, what on earth is this—a stockmarket board?"

The young man grinned. "Yes, Mrs. Oss, this is our cigarette stock exchange. Would you be interested?" he joked.

"Cigarette exchange?" Really, now. That was hard to believe. Yet she knew that the Red Cross packages had contained cigarettes. In fact, when she and John had received theirs they had wondered what they would do with them.

Some of the missionaries had tied their bundles of cigarettes to a brick and dropped them into the stream. When the water dissolved the paper and glue, the tobacco floated to the top. A group of men walking by spotted the floating tobacco.

"Who did that?" yelled one with indignation. "They're crazy, throwing away cigarettes!" Wading into the water, he scooped up the wet tobacco as though it were a precious find.

"Let me have some," called one of the group.

"I want some too," shouted another.

"This tobacco is mine," the first man said angrily. Seconds later the three men were fist fighting, until someone warned them what would happen if the guards caught them.

So this was the commodity now being exchanged on the prison "Wall Street" board. Olga wished it had been powdered milk or cheese and that she could have purchased several shares for John.

Since coming to camp, John's health had not been good. A recent bout with dysentery and lack of proper nutrition had caused it to steadily decline. His stomach could not endure the worm-laden oatmeal and rice and the coarse vegetables. John was slowly starving. One of the camp doctors had examined him and declared that he ought actually to be in a hospital.

Olga was sure that the commandant would not allow him to be taken to a hospital. Only those who became critically ill and could neither eat nor walk were taken to the Japanese-controlled hospitals in Shanghai. They were most careful to see that no one died in camp, lest this record bring retaliation on the Japanese interned in the United States.

Without medication and nourishing food, the inevitable day finally came when John could not rally enough strength even to swallow. The doctors in camp could do nothing for him. Olga, in charge also of the infirmary on second floor, sent a report to the commandant, who sent the Japanese doctor to examine him.

"He must be taken to an outside hospital," was the decision.

"Where?" Olga questioned.

No reply. Now doubts began to fill her mind. Where would they take John? Would they really take him to a hospital, or would they take him away to die? Maybe even kill him? Suddenly panic gripped her. If anything happened to John, how could she go on?

Olga left the infirmary to search for the man in charge of men's affairs. "Lenny, will they really take John to a hospital, or will they get rid of him?" Her voice broke.

Lenny looked glum. "I really don't know, Olga. I wish we could trust them. Look, if they hurt your husband, I'll kill them. In fact, I found some gas pipes in the junk pile. I've got them hidden. We could hit the guards over the head and kill them if they took your husband away."

Horrified, Olga begged, "Oh, no, no, no! We mustn't do anything like that. We'll have to let John go and trust God to take care of him." She didn't try to hold back the tears.

Very shortly a Chinese driver brought his taxicab to a halt inside the camp. An armed guard came immediately and stood by the car. When Olga saw the cab, she wanted to cry, "My husband needs an ambulance, not a cab!" But she was silent.

Moments later the screams of a little girl could be heard all the way from the infirmary. The girl, badly undernourished and suffering from starved nerve endings, was being carried to the car. Every slight movement caused excruciating pain.

And only that morning, a two-year-old boy had accidentally fallen into a pan of hot water and scalded his little body. Now this screaming, hysterical tot was also brought out of the infirmary and placed in the car. His parents sobbed uncontrollably.

The girl with the starved nerve endings could not tolerate sitting or lying down. Her screams echoing throughout the camp caused Olga's blood to chill.

Finally they carried John to the cab and placed the little boy on his lap. John made an attempt to fold his arms around the child, but they fell helpless to his side. He was unable to respond to Olga's embrace and could speak no words of comfort.

The cab started abruptly, carrying the shrieking girl, the screaming child, and John past the double row of barbed wire, and out through the iron gates. Those who watched cried at the sight—the rough taxi bumping over the ruts with its screaming cargo of humans.

When John left, Olga felt that she had lost a part of herself. His words of cheer, his refusal to be discouraged, his unwavering faith in God, had been her daily strength. Now her companion was gone.

Bowing her head and crying unashamedly, she prayed, "Dear God, unto Thy care I commit Thy servant. May Thy angels be ever by his side. I pray for strength to carry on without him."

6—B.B.W.

Behind Barbed Wire

The taxi clunked along over the rough roads and through the streets of Shanghai, finally coming to a halt before the General Hospital. The two children had never stopped screaming. Now they were taken away by hospital attendants. Weak as he was, John made note of the Japanese guards patrolling the hospital premises with fixed bayonets on their rifles. Unable to walk by himself, he had to be carried. Attendants carried him to the top floor, which had been reserved for prisoners of war. After they placed him in a bed and shut the door, he sank at once into the detached world of oblivion.

Hours later he opened his eyes and glanced around the room. Where was he? Then he remembered. They had taken him from camp to this hospital. He was in the prison ward. He thought of Olga. How sad she had looked. Lifting his thoughts, he prayed that God would care for his wife and give her courage and strength.

The door opened and the pleasant face of a Chinese nurse met his eyes. "Mr. Oss," she spoke kindly, "I wonder if you realize that you are in this hospital as a prisoner of war. The Japanese are in control. They have their guards all over the place. We must be very careful and obey their commands."

"Yes," John's reply came weakly.

The nurse smiled, and held out a piece of paper. "The commandant from the Chapei Civilian Assembly Center, where you were interned, has asked that you sign this statement. Let me read it for you:

" 'When you are permitted release to an outside hospital, you are strictly prohibited from communicating with any outside person. You are not permitted the following:

1. To contact any visitors.
2. To send or receive any letters.
3. To use the telephone.
4. To get anyone to buy anything for you.

" 'You must remember that the authorities have ways and means of checking on any occurrence or action by you that may be contrary to the rules and regulations of the Japanese government. . . .

" 'Violators will be subject to severe punishment.' "

John listened with dread to the harsh rules, but could not raise his hand to sign the statement. The nurse assisted him by guiding his hand, as he made a weak scrawl.

In the hospital, some medication was provided, and John felt his strength returning. But the food situation was only a little better than at camp. Each morning the attendants brought him the inevitable oatmeal. Even if the "raisins" were missing, he could not stomach oatmeal anymore. For supper a cold potato and a piece of meat was the unvaried fare. He ate the potato, but left the meat. The animal flesh, if diseased, would only endanger his health further. But now he felt the pangs of real hunger.

A talkative Filipino patient shared his room. At first all John could do was to smile at his loquacious room partner. Gradually, as his strength returned, he conversed with him.

The Filipino said, "You say your name is John Oss, and you are an ordained minister. I think I heard you preach once at the Y.M.C.A. in Shanghai—on Tibet Road."

Propping himself on his arm, John showed his interest. "Yes, I remember preaching a sermon there once. Were you in the congregation?"

"You're a Seventh-day Adventist missionary, aren't you?"

"That's right," John replied. "And I was editor for our publishing house in Shanghai. We printed the *Signs of the Times*."

"Wonderful," beamed the Filipino. "And I know your conference president, Pastor Hsu Hwa."

"Oh, you do? I wonder where he is now."

Suddenly the Filipino spoke with an undertone. "My name is Macario Ochabe. You can trust me. Do you want to get in touch with him? I can call him and give a message for you."

"But I would not want to break any rules. Besides, it might get you in trouble."

"Bah! We're not breaking any rules. The Japanese trust me.

They let me go in and out of this place. I'll call Pastor Hsu Hwa and just tell him you're a patient in this hospital. Maybe he can come to see you and help you."

John brightened. "Well, that would be all right."

When the lights went off suddenly, the two men continued to talk into the night. John was encouraged.

When several days had passed and he felt stronger, John was able to rise from his bed and take a few steps. One morning he was determined to exercise his legs by trying to walk down the hall. Slowly he advanced and then paused at the end of the hall before a glass door overlooking the hospital entrance. A terrible weakness almost prostrated him. Leaning against the door, he asked himself, "Could it be that I am going to die after all from lack of proper nourishment?"

He closed his eyes and rested. When he opened them again and glanced outside through the glass door, he saw something below that almost caused his weak heart to stop beating.

A ricksha had pulled to a stop in front of the hospital. A woman with a familiar face—dressed in a very familiar gray squirrel coat —stepped out. Instantly John recognized the face. It was Mrs. Laing. He could never forget how Olga had persuaded her not to take her life with the deadly opium in the silver box. Mrs. Laing had spent the last night of freedom with them. Now *why* was she *here?* What would she do?

All sorts of wild thoughts raced through his mind, bringing horror. "Could it be that she has come to see me? Dear God, if she seeks me out, the Japanese will think I am a spy. They will harm her—maybe even kill her!" He was not concerned so much for himself as for her. "Dear God, don't let her try to see me."

As he stood galvanized on the spot, he hoped that she would look up, so that he could signal to her. He would urge her to go away. Mrs. Laing did not look up. Instead, she walked boldly into the building. The guards' footsteps and a clatter of sudden activity heightened his heartbeat. Looking around, he sought a way to hide.

Then he remembered that if he tried to hide, the guards might indeed become suspicious. Helpless to stem the tide of events, he found suddenly that the thing he greatly feared had come upon him.

Mrs. Laing came upstairs and walked briskly down the hall in his direction. Then she saw him standing by the door. Smiling broadly, she approached him and held out a dainty hand, American fashion. She spoke almost casually.

"And how is Mr. Oss today?" She pretended not to notice that he was trembling, and sweating profusely.

John glanced around wildly. "How did you get past the guards? You must not stay, Mrs. Laing."

Ignoring his concern, she pulled a little white envelope out of her squirrel muff and quietly slipped it into his hand. John, still petrified, shoved the envelope into his dressing-gown pocket.

"Mrs. Laing, you shouldn't—"

Before he could finish, she flashed a sweet smile, turned as suddenly as she had come, and vanished. Now a barrage of questions agitated his brain. How did she know he was here? How did she get past the guards? Why did she come? What was in the envelope?

Shuffling as fast as his weak legs could carry him, he reached his room and fell on the bed. Resting a moment, he reached into his pocket for the envelope and tore it open. He gasped at what he saw. This was unbelievable! But it was true. Here in his hands, a gift from that angel woman of the silver opium box, was 10,000 yen. A quick calculation told him it amounted to $250 in American currency. God had sent help. Now he could get his Filipino friend to buy the medicines he needed and the food his body cried for.

A few days later Macario was given permission to leave the hospital, fortified with the money John had given him. Once out, he telephoned Pastor Hsu Hwa and told him that John Oss was a prisoner in the General Hospital, desperately needing medication and food.

The very next day Pastor Hsu Hwa went to the hospital and requested permission to visit, not John Oss, but Macario Ochabe. He was allowed to visit him.

Once in the room, Pastor Hsu Hwa gave John no recognition, giving Macario the opportunity to introduce them. He addressed himself only to the Filipino. The conversation went naturally to food and vitamins and medicines.

"How I would love some cottage cheese and milk," John put in.

Pastor Hsu Hwa showed no emotion, no sign that he had heard. Turning to his new-found Filipino friend, he promised, "I'll come back next visiting day."

On his next visit he carried some packages into the hospital, and somehow managed to get them through, stating that they were for Macario Ochabe. The girl at the desk did not probe. So he hurried to the room. "Here, Macario, put these under the bed," he urged.

After Pastor Hsu Hwa left, Macario whispered to John, "There's food in these packages. I'll take them to the men's room. Follow me, and I'll see that you get some."

And so John Oss, suffering from malnutrition, slid off his bed, followed his friend to the men's room, and ate. There were the cottage cheese and the milk. And though he was no cake eater, he consumed even the sweet cake that Pastor Hsu Hwa had brought, eating tiny portions at first. In the days that followed, Macario slipped out, as often as he dared, with money in his pocket, returning always with food and vitamin pills. Somehow the guards remained unsuspecting.

John Oss ate and lived. Shortly after, because of his rapid recovery, the doctors issued an order for his return to prison camp. John praised God with a full heart and serenity of mind, unafraid of the days ahead. Had not God, in his hour of greatest need, sent an angel in the form of Mrs. Laing to care for him?

And now he looked forward with joyful expectation. He would see his beloved Olga again.

Worms and Woes | 11

Six weeks after he had left, John found himself back in the prison camp. Though now the pulse of life flowed stronger through his veins, new threats of disease awaited him. An epidemic of dysentery swept through the camp. Hundreds of men, women, and children had already taken to their beds. Scores filled the overcrowded infirmary. Only a few, who had escaped the disease and were able to stand on their feet, assisted the sick.

Adding to everyone's distress were swarms of mosquitoes that filled the humid summer air. Some prisoners were fortunate enough to have brought nets, which they now hung around their beds. But the majority continued to be plagued by the pests, even unavoidably breathing them into their nostrils at times. Many years in China had made Olga a little more foresighted than some. She searched her trunk and found a can of Flit. Asking everyone who could, to leave the room, she sprayed the air. The mosquitos fell by the thousands. Swept up from the floor, they filled a fair-sized jar. Someone suggested that it should be presented to the commandant.

Olga decided she would be the brave one. Perhaps he would do something to correct the intolerable situation. But she failed in this venture. The commandant, apparently unmoved by what was only a natural condition in this part of the world, did nothing. Mosquitoes continued to fill the air, inside and out.

Prisoners lucky enough to end up in the infirmary fared a little better on food. It became a real privilege to be admitted.

One morning when Olga made her rounds in the infirmary, she was surprised to find Mrs. Jones there again. This lady, her hair dyed blond but now streaked with natural brown, lay in a bed resting comfortably, but her face appeared flushed. Everyone knew that pudgy Mrs. Jones shirked her duties and loved to lie in bed. Her complaints were endless, and few failed to notice her friendliness with the guards. As Olga walked around the room taking temperatures, she wondered. How did *she* manage to get into the infirmary so often? What was her ailment? When she came to Mrs. Jones, she quietly slipped a thermometer under her tongue. It read 105 degrees. Calling the volunteer nurse, she whispered, "Mrs. Jones has a high fever. Watch her closely."

On her next round, the nurse came to Olga and whispered, "May I speak privately with you?"

"Of course." She wondered why the nurse seemed so evasive.

"I know why Mrs. Jones had a temperature of 105 degrees. I caught her placing the thermometer on the hot water bottle."

Olga was not a bit surprised. "All right, we'll take the matter to the superintendent."

Exposed by her own craftiness, Mrs. Jones soon found herself in the kitchen peeling potatoes.

The camp's roster contained the names of eleven doctors, all prisoners of war. These men, with a meager supply of medicines, mostly aspirin, treated those who were ill. Few supplies came through the Red Cross now. Dr. Hunza, himself a victim of cancer, devoted his failing strength to treating the sick. The Dutch doctor, hardly able to stand on his feet, and fully aware that it was only a matter of time before cancer would take his life, never wavered in his duties.

While hundreds of prisoners fell victim to disease, Olga had thus far managed to escape. She was able therefore to wait on others, spending every waking moment between the kitchen and the infirmary. John, now back with her, spent his days also helping the sick, until one morning he could not get out of bed. All the symptoms pointed to dysentery. Day after day he lay ill, losing precious strength.

Olga hovered over him, determined that she would nurse him back to health. John responded, and was soon on his feet again, until the middle of one night, when they rushed him and Olga and others to the infirmary, victims of ptomaine poisoning. Weakened by this new disorder, John again contracted dysentery, and continued to have one attack after another, until finally he was left irreparably weak.

While Olga worried over John, she found herself suddenly losing weight with alarming rapidity. Her dress hung from her shoulders like a tent. Feeling her sunken cheeks and noticing her bony fingers and skinny legs, she felt a secret dread. What could be wrong now?

Illness of every kind swept through the camp. Malnutrition became boldly apparent. Children walked about on little toothpick legs, whining and crying for food. None received the 1,200 calories required by international law. The rice and soybeans were dirty, hulled, unpalatable. Those who came to camp overweight were now mere shadows. Even Mr. Krug could now twist and turn in bed without a squeak from his once-protesting cot.

Then, even worse than the dysentery, another horrifying experience came to Olga. She discovered that her nose seemed to be turning into a block of ice! And strange shivers slipped up and down her spine, followed by an uncontrollable shaking. Placing her hands on her heart, she felt wild pounding. Her secret dread turned into cold panic. She was going to be ill—terribly ill.

Her first thought was to find John. Leaving the camp kitchen, she found John coming from the unyielding vegetable garden. She observed his colorless face and almost decided she had better not worry him. But she could not hide from him her shaking body, nor drive away the terrible chills.

John noticed her trembling. "Olga, dear, you're not getting sick?" He placed a supporting arm around her shaking body. A worried crease lined his face.

"I'm afraid so, dear. Will you help me to the room?" Olga

leaned on John's arm as he led her to the room and helped her gently into bed, piling all the bedding he could find on her shaking body. He left and returned shortly with a hot water bottle. Kissing her, he left to find a doctor. "I'll be back shortly," he assured her.

Moments later he returned with Dr. Hunza, whose sunken face revealed that cancer was consuming his body. The doctor sat on the bed and examined Olga. He said nothing until he rose and faced them. Then with a tired voice he sighed, "Malaria. We'll give her quinine and keep her in bed."

With the infirmary full, Olga remained in her own bed, with John assisting her as much as he could. Recuperation was slow. Proper nourishment was not available. Eventually, however, she recovered, but the continued lack of good food and medicines made her an easy prey to subsequent attacks. Altogether she contracted malaria six times while in the prison camp.

Right after her first bout with malaria, another illness dealt a blow. This time she felt the current of life ebbing from her veins. There was no shaking, only a draining debilitation. She took her own temperature, and finding it abnormally low, decided that this time it could not be malaria.

Again John summoned Dr. Hunza. His thin fingers felt her pulse. "No fever," he muttered weakly. Turning to John, he asked, "Can you get a basin?"

"I'll try," John said and hurried out, returning with one almost immediately.

"Now, Olga, put your finger in your throat and try to make yourself vomit," the doctor ordered.

Olga looked up, completely puzzled. But she complied, slowly poking a finger down her throat. Immediately she felt herself gagging. With very little effort, up came some fluid, followed by something that looked like a white string. The doctor reached into the basin and held up the thirteen-inch "string." "I thought so—worms!" he muttered.

Olga gasped and shuddered. "Oh, no, doctor! How can I live with worms inside of me?" Unrestrainable tears accompanied the outburst.

Smiling weakly, the doctor said, "Why are you crying? I have worms. *Everyone* in China has worms!"

Pointing to a red line on the worm's underside, he said, "Now listen, this happens to be a male. Chances are you won't have any more. The fact that you had no food inside your stomach made this worm come up. He's starved. And you are not the only one in camp with worms. All the children have them. We expect some worm medicine soon from the Red Cross."

Olga prayed that the worm medicine would arrive soon. It did, and the doctors passed it out to all the people.

Some teased her about the worms. "Do you have a hatchery?" they asked. After she had swallowed the worm medicine, she found she could laugh safely with the teasers.

It came easy for her to be pleasant, until one day another affliction seized her. While showering she noticed an ugly red rash starting at the rib cage and circling her body. A terrible itching along with the rash maddened her.

Again Dr. Hunza came to her rescue. "Shingles this time," he announced.

"Shingles?" Olga's tone voiced a question mark.

"This is a disease of the nervous system. You are not alone in this either," consoled the doctor. "We have many, many cases in camp."

Olga looked at the doctor's sunken face, now completely colorless, and compassion filled her heart. Ill as the doctor was, he did not neglect to assist her as well as he could during the next six weeks, while the skin was almost unbearably tender.

When finally she recovered from the shingles, she found herself with very little strength. John, who had nursed her, again fell ill himself, and Olga used her remaining strength to care for him in turn.

Then came the day when sad news flashed across the camp. Dr. Hunza was dead. Cancer had won. Keen sorrow was felt by all who had watched the suffering, dedicated physician serve others so unselfishly.

John and Olga were filled with sadness. Yet they could be grateful too. They were being severely chastised, but they were still alive. Like Job, they could praise God for sparing them to carry out His plans for them—plans which under the circumstances they could but dimly understand.

12 | War News Leaks Out

Summer months slipped away. Autumn's first frosty mornings brought added discomfort to the prisoners in the camp's unheated rooms. Winter followed, spreading a merciless chill in the air and adding to everyone's misery.

At two o'clock one cold morning a guard ran through the halls pounding on doors and yelling, "You will gather for roll call. The commandant has ordered a roll call."

Covers flew off the beds, and one by one people hustled to obey. Olga shivered. What could the commandant want now—at this early hour? In a moment she stood in line beside her husband along with all the others. The door sprang open, and the commandant—fully dressed—strutted into the hall. All bowed low. Glaring at the shivering, bewildered group, he spat his angry words, "We have received word that four of our Japanese in American prison camps have been KILL—ED." His eyes flashed with hot anger.

Olga wanted to slip to the floor. She leaned toward John. What would the enemy do now? Would he retaliate? Were they going to be shot, after all?

The commandant continued, face livid with rage, "If we get word like this again, we will SHOOT YOU. Do you understand? We will SHOOT ALL OF YOU." As though unable to control himself any longer, he turned abruptly and left.

Although they were allowed to return to their rooms, for the rest of the night few could sleep. They discussed the incident in deep undertones, wondering if the commandant's threats would be carried out.

But the monotony of camp life soon took over again. Lack of food and the many inconveniences resulting from living in close proximity to one another were beginning to affect everyone, depressing some and irritating others. Men swore loosely, even gambling and shouting threats upon losing. Tempers flared without excuse. Even the children whined and cried more frequently.

One morning a loud noise from the west building sent Olga running to investigate. One of her duties was to check and report to the superintendent any unusual behavior. Now it appeared that an ugly brawl had erupted between Mrs. Wentworth, an immaculate housekeeper, and Mrs. Carrie, one considerably less meticulous. Mrs. Wentworth was forever scrubbing the floor next to her bed. Mrs. Carrie, on the other hand, spent most of her time in bed, cursing over trivial matters.

This morning Mrs. Wentworth's eternal cleaning had irked Mrs. Carrie beyond endurance, and she exploded.

"Will you quit scrubbing that floor? You must be an awful dirty person, having to clean all the time like you do!"

Without warning Mrs. Wentworth rose to her feet and tossed the bucket of dirty water at the unsuspecting woman, pouring the filthy liquid over her head.

Olga walked in just in time to witness the dripping Mrs. Carrie pulling Mrs. Wentworth's long hair, and screaming, "You dirty pig—you—" While attempting to separate the two incensed women, she received a few blows herself.

"Come on now, ladies, you must stop this kind of behavior. We aren't going to be behind barbed wires forever," she consoled. "Besides, you are playing into the enemy's hands."

There was no reconciling the two women. Only by shifting beds around and separating them could peace be restored.

Life in the barbed-wire prison was a lonely existence—like being in an underground tunnel, with the black unknown surrounding them. After the first few weeks in camp, even the Shanghai *North Star* newspaper ceased to be available. Now the only news that reached the prisoners was in clippings that the Japanese posted daily on the wall. These always reported Japanese victories, telling of fantastic success in their island-hopping conquest of the Pacific. According to this propaganda, the Americans were suffering incalculable losses, and it was only a matter of time before the United States itself would be in the hands of the Japanese. Things looked blacker every day, and the morale of the prisoners sank to an all-time low.

The air was quiet one Sabbath afternoon when John and Olga slipped away from the others and walked toward the stream at the edge of the camp. They hoped to spend a few hours of quiet by themselves. Reaching the edge of the stream, they watched the guards patrol between the two rows of barbed wire. Back and forth they marched, guns with fixed bayonets at the ready. A pall seemed to hang heavy over the camp.

A sudden swish of water from the stream caught the Osses' attention. At the same time a young man whom they recognized as John Tall, a wealthy prisoner (all his wealth being on the outside), came strolling by. He motioned for them to be quiet. Olga held her breath. Why was he so secretive? The guard was close by.

The water splashed gently, and a swift movement came from the wild grass along the stream's edge. They watched the guard, but he had not noticed. Suddenly a head bobbed out of the water. The swimmer was a young boy—a Chinese. He spoke hurriedly to John Tall, who stepped closer to the stream and stood hidden among the reeds. They could not hear the conversation.

"What do you suppose that boy is here for?" Olga asked.

"Let's be quiet, Olga. We'll soon find out."

The young man reappeared and walked toward them. "Shhh—" His voice was a whisper. "We have friends on the outside who bring us news of the war. The Russians have held Stalingrad and the Germans have retreated. Russia is our ally, so that means victory for our side. Whoopee!" he whistled under his breath. A wide grin covered his handsome face.

Joy flooded their hearts. News of the Americans at last. And victory too! Olga squeezed John's hand. She wanted to kiss the bearer of good news! Unable to restrain a burst of gratitude, she cried, "Oh, thank You, God." John smiled and was about to speak.

But the young man placed a finger to his lips. "None of this to anyone yet. I'll inform the superintendent. He will find a way to circulate the news among the people."

"Don't worry. Not a word from us," Olga promised.

The happy young man bounded away with his good news. Besides the young swimmer, the contact provided by the underground, another channel opened up through which news of American victories seeped into camp. During the many months of internment, Olga had never forgotten her promise to look after Anna, the fourteen-year-old girl who had claimed American citizenship as a result of being born at sea. Olga remembered the girl's distraught parents that day at the Country Club, and she had taken Anna under her wing. They became good friends, and Anna often confided in Olga, telling her once that she had a sweetheart on the outside in Shanghai. The boy was a White Russian whose family had fled their native land after the Communist take-over and had settled in China. The girl's eyes had sparkled when she told Olga, "Papow promised me that he would keep in touch with me."

Smiling indulgently, Olga had said, "Well, dear, he will find a way." They took walks together, often circling the inside path of the barbed wires and talking about the day when they would be on the outside. Always the guards marched back and forth, back and forth.

They were walking past the chemical plant located right in the middle of the camp, one day, when they caught the melody of a singing voice coming from the plant. The voice came strong and vibrant. They slowed down to listen to the singing. Suddenly a face appeared at the window. Seeing the face, Anna jumped up and down bursting with elation. "There he is, Olga! There's my sweetheart! There's Papow!"

In a flash Olga saw the plot. The young man had indeed found a way. Somehow he had secured a job in the Japanese chemical plant so he could be near his sweetheart. She was happy for the girl; but, oh, they must not let the guards become suspicious.

"Anna, be calm. Act as though nothing has happened. Do not show recognition. If the guards see this, they might kill him." She gripped the girl's arm to hold her still. But Anna wanted to get closer to the fence that circled the chemical plant. Olga pulled her back. "Remember, dear, the Japanese have warned us that the fence is electrified."

Anna stopped suddenly and looked at her sweetheart standing clearly in the window and singing lustily. Tears of joy spilled down her smooth cheeks. "Oh, if only I could talk with him," she cried.

"Come on, Anna, we must keep walking. The guards will surely notice if we stand still."

"But, Olga, he's singing in Russian and trying to tell us something."

"All right, let's just walk very slowly then so we can hear what he's saying."

They took a few slow steps. "What is he saying?" Olga asked.

The girl's pretty face beamed. "Olga, he's giving us the war news. He's singing about the American victories. The Americans are making many gains. Maybe we'll be liberated soon." The girl cried and laughed with constrained joy.

"The Japanese can't understand Russian," Anna burst out.

"No, and I can't either," Olga replied. Her stomach was turning somersaults for joy. Out loud she said, "Oh, thank God. Thank God." Again taking the girl's arm, she urged, "Now let us walk back quite naturally. Let's find Mr. Drew and give him the news. And John, too, will be so happy to know."

Soon the good news popped around the camp. And day after day, while the guards posted news of Japanese victories, Olga and Anna strolled past the chemical plant and listened to the singing sweetheart. Latent hope stirred anew in their hearts. Anna's won-

7—B.B.W.

derful singing sweetheart had dispelled the gloom. And the un-suspecting guards kept on marching back and forth.

Olga and John looked forward to the Sabbath. Even in this prison camp, the Sabbath hours brought them a measure of peace and rest. No one objected when they slipped away to seek solitude and quiet among the trees and bushes near the stream. Here they worshiped God, unmolested by the stir of the camp. John always read from the Bible. His faith never wavered, and his courage never dimmed. They communed with the Creator and prayed. Especially were they thankful that the prejudice that at first had been shown toward them had been dispelled. Now they were highly regarded, and John was sought for his religious ministry.

On a Sabbath afternoon when the hot winds of a second sum-mer behind barbed wires blew through camp, John and Olga sat near the stream reading their Bible. Suddenly they noticed the guards on duty acting strange. They were running helter-skelter throughout the camp, wildly waving their pistols in the air and shouting orders. Prisoners came running from every direction to hear what they were saying.

"Go to your rooms. Do not walk around camp. Do not look out of the windows. We will shoot anyone who does not obey," came the shouts.

Convinced by the pistols, all, including John and Olga, hurried to their rooms. A moment later, out of the fleecy white clouds, came the faintest murmur of engines. Olga and John sat on their beds, eyes turned toward the window. No one moved, or even spoke a word. Suddenly there came the cracking of pistols. The guards were firing their guns. The murmur of engines grew louder and louder, obviously a squadron of planes approaching.

Eyes zigzagged in every direction. None dared to venture near the window. But now, anxiety gave place to slow smiles and glow-ing eyes. These must be American planes. Else why were the guards so angry?

Then a horrifying thought came to Olga. What if they bombed

the chemical plant? She recalled the words of the commandant that first day in camp. "If the Americans bomb this place, you will all die."

John, unruffled, sat quietly on his bed, smiling at his wife, not guessing the terror in her heart. No one stirred as the planes' roar reached a crescendo over the camp. From their point of observation all watched as tiny bits of shining, aluminum-like paper floated in the air. What could they be? Perhaps messages from the Americans? They would never get to see them. The guards would see to that. Later they learned that the tiny bits of aluminum had been used by the American planes as means of anti-radar detection.

Then as suddenly as they had arrived, the roaring planes disappeared. The sound of cracking pistols could still be heard throughout the silent camp. Now someone was saying, "They were American planes. They came to encourage us. Perhaps soon we will be liberated." Gurgles of joy could not be suppressed.

After this event, the guards looked upon all movements in camp with suspicion. Olga and Anna had to be more careful during their strolls. A large pile of rubble, uncleared after the bombing of the university many months before, remained in camp. Olga searched for a few pieces of coke one morning to start a fire in her little firepot, since the Japanese now provided no fuel for private cooking or heating.

As she scratched around in the rubble, she heard the roar of an engine directly overhead. The sound almost knocked her weak knees from under her. The plane suddenly made a dive and flew so low that she saw the pilot's face—definitely an American face! The pilot threw a hat, and it landed right in the pile of rubble. She actually saw the American symbol and the number of the plane. The pilot waved to her wildly. Two men walking nearby saw him wave also. As the plane circled the camp, Olga thought her heart would burst from excitement and joy. John, wherever he was, must have seen it too.

The plane seemed to turn into a large, graceful, friendly bird as it continued to swoop and circle overhead. Olga was unprepared for what came next. The Japanese opened fire on the plane with machine guns. Olga tried to stop her heart from galloping when she realized that the Japanese had machine guns buried right in camp, probably nests of them. She almost fell to the ground from weakness.

Instantly the American pilot retaliated with his machine gun and then quickly vanished into the fluffy clouds.

Olga hurried back to her room. Again the order was issued, "Do not leave your rooms." While the guards could force obedience to this command, they could not stifle jubilation within the hearts of the prisoners. They also could not keep it a secret that three guards, either wounded or killed, had been carried away on stretchers.

Starvation Threatens | 13

Although new hope for liberation now filled the hearts of the prisoners, Olga began to fear more and more that John would not live to see that day. One attack after another of dysentery left him without strength. New symptoms kept appearing. The diet, now reduced to one bowl of plain soybeans per day, without oil, salt, or any kind of seasoning, did not tempt John. Others, who before had eaten even worms and weevils with their food, could not be tempted either.

At first there had been the gnawing hunger pangs. Then stomachs had shrunk, and the hunger pangs left. Later the stomachs swelled and became hard. Even the children, who before had cried for food, refused the soybeans placed before them. Most of the children had worms. The white strings hung from their bowels as they walked around camp. Yet few appeared ruffled. Mothers simply pulled the worms out of the passive children.

As the days passed and American victories became more frequent, the attitude of the Japanese toward their prisoners hardened, and they seemed determined to make life more uncomfortable than ever. The day came when an order was issued: No more hot water for baths or dishwashing. From the beginning the drinking water had to be boiled. Now even this cautionary measure was prohibited. Without soap and hot water, the layers of dirt, grease, and grime in the kitchen, bathrooms, and dormitories became thicker and thicker.

To add to the internees' uneasiness, news filtered through camp that the Americans in Japanese prison camps in Manila were suffering heavily. Rumors had it that many were desperately ill and starving, that a number had been shot, and that the rest were doomed to die also.

Clearly they saw that unless the war ended soon, the Japanese would starve them too, unless God intervened—right here in the Chapei Civilian Assembly Center.

John's body, day by day ravaged by amoebic dysentery, yielded to the disease, and he began to lapse intermittently into unconsciousness. Several prison doctors examined him. Turning to Olga, one doctor said, "Without medication, we can do nothing. Unless he gets to a hospital and receives treatment, he will die." Then he shook his head, "The Japanese are not allowing anyone to leave now."

Olga bent over John's unconscious form, crying, "But what is wrong with him besides the dysentery? What makes him lapse into unconsciousness?"

The doctors, unable to make any further diagnosis, could not reply. Occasionally John would open his eyes and look at his wife, and she would plead, "John, speak to me. Tell me what is wrong."

No words came. A moment later his eyes would close and he would fall back into the world of oblivion.

Two weeks passed. Terrified by the knowledge that John might die, Olga determined to go personally to the commandant and request that he be sent to an outside hospital. Anyplace was better than here, where nobody could do anything but stand helplessly by.

She realized that it would take a lot of sheer buzz-saw nerve to approach the commandant with her request. Whenever he spoke to the prisoners now his voice was angry and vindictive. And it seemed that the guards fondled their guns with itchy fingers. She realized, of course, that they were furious because of the American victories. She decided that, furious or no, she would go to him and plead for her husband's life.

Early the next morning she approached the guard standing before the commandant's office. Boldly she stated her business, "I wish to see Mr. Tsuruki. I must see him. My husband is dying."

The guard's small, frosty eyes met hers. "No!" came the fierce reply. "Go back to your room."

"Please, please, you know the international law. A seriously ill prisoner—" The look of contempt on his face stopped her. "Dear God," she thought, "what can I do now?"

"You *must* let me see the commandant. My husband may die." She brushed the hot tears away. Oh, she mustn't cry before these men.

Suddenly the unexpected happened. The guard changed his mind and escorted her before the commandant. As she stood before the small officious figure, a wave of weakness coursed through her body. She thought she would faint. Then she forced herself to stand steady on her thin legs. She *must* plead for her husband. If John died, what did it matter what became of her? A surge of courage rose to meet her need.

"Mr. Tsuruki, I came to tell you that my husband is very, very ill. Several of the doctors have examined him and cannot diagnose his illness."

Mr. Tsuruki appeared unimpressed. "Is he in pain?"

"No. That's not it. He is not in pain, but keeps losing consciousness. And of course, he can't eat."

A snicker came from the commandant.

"If he is not in pain, and the doctors have no diagnosis, then he cannot leave this camp."

Olga could not subdue the wild gallop of her heart. The frantic words spilled out, "But, Mr. Tsuruki, must one be in pain to be seriously ill? The doctors have said he will die if he does not go to a hospital."

His next words almost sent her reeling to the ground.

"This is WAR! We cannot send out every patient who feels like sleeping all the time."

Desperately Olga pleaded, "But he isn't sleeping. He is unconscious."

Suddenly something crystallized in her mind. One reason why

the commandant hesitated to send a prisoner out to the hospital was that he could easily return with the news of American victories. She had to find a good argument to convince. A silent prayer found its way to the heavenly courts. Then came the answer.

With a brazen thrust she delivered her argument, "Mr. Tsuruki, you are aware that according to international law any critically ill prisoner must be removed to a hospital." Pausing for a second, she continued, "You realize, of course, that if my husband died in this camp, it would not look well for you."

The commandant tightened his lips. And he looked frightfully angry, as though he could not believe the audacity of her words. He turned away from her and spat. "Bring me a statement from the doctor." And Olga was dismissed.

Moments later she returned with a doctor's statement, which read:

"John Oss requires medical treatment which we are unable to give in this camp. Unless hospitalized at once, imminent death must result."

Now the commandant was convinced. He ordered John Oss's removal from camp. After her husband was taken away, a horrible suspicion assailed Olga's mind. What if they did not take him to a hospital? Mustering all her nerve again she went to the commandant to ask, "Will you tell me where my husband has been sent to?"

This time there was no yielding.

"Mrs. Oss, we positively cannot release any information regarding your husband. You will go to your room and not come back again with your demands."

"But I have a right to know where my husband is."

"No. You have no more rights." His eyes flashed with hot anger. "You will leave now."

Sick at heart, she turned and left the room. Trembling and tottering, she made her way to her room and collapsed on the bed, sobbing into her pillow.

Food Falls From Heaven | 14

As the days slowly passed, it seemed to Olga that each one slipped into nothingness. What would tomorrow hold? Food continued to be scarce. Even the garden plot, famished for want of fertilizer, refused to yield. And with the daily ration of food having been reduced to one cup of soybeans for each prisoner, stark signs of malnutrition appeared everywhere. Even the bread, which had been dragged in on carts by coolies, with dirty delivery boys sitting on top of the unwrapped loaves, was cut off. It was just as well, Olga told herself. For inside the loaves one was apt to find stones, hulls of all kinds, and baked-in vermin. One day when someone soaked a loaf, it turned into a gooey, indescribable mess and later hardened like concrete.

Whatever physical problems beset the prisoners, overweight was not one of them. Those who had arrived at camp with extra poundage found reducing as easy as magic.

The infirmary was always full, and one morning as Olga went about her duties, she heard strange cries coming from the hallway. Stepping out to investigate, she almost bumped into a young man who in the early days of camp had always been a chow hound and well-padded with body weight. Now waving his thin arms in the air, he was running and yelling, "No food for me! No food for me!" Mr. Drew ran after him, trying to catch him.

Olga noted how his clothes now flapped in the breeze like the loose drapings of a scarecrow on a windy day, and she sympathized. Poor man; food had meant so much to him. It appeared to her that the fellow might be losing his mind.

The young man was eventually cornered and confined to the

"crazy room." Day and night his cries continued to pierce the air, "No food for me! No food for me!"

Sometimes the prisoners gathered and excited their imaginations with talk of gastronomic delights. Invariably the conversation went like this: "What will be the very first thing you will do when you get out?"

And almost everyone would reply, "I want to eat a whole cake, or a whole pie, or a big, thick filet mignon."

When Olga was asked what she would like, she replied, "I want to see my husband."

"No, no, we're talking about food."

"Oh," answered Olga. "I want a Hershey bar most of all."

At seven o'clock one morning Olga gathered a small bundle of soiled laundry and headed for the trough where running water was provided for washing clothes. She walked slowly. Always of slender build, she now was very frail. Her legs were thin and always bare. Only a few women still had hose to wear, and her own had long since worn to shreds. With dollar-sized holes in her shoes, her feet hurt almost constantly. Her wardrobe now consisted of one thin voile dress, the shoes on her feet, and very little else.

This morning was particularly cheerless. Those stirring around the camp all wore dejection on their faces. Only the day before, a Shanghai typhoon had whipped through the area, strewing havoc everywhere. Even now a stubborn wind remained to chill the air. Olga shivered. Camp morale, her own included, seemed at an all-time low. Around the camp, rumors flew fast and thick. Some said the Japanese were winning the war, and all internees would be killed any day now. Others maintained that the Americans had made tremendous advances. Oh, the agony, the torture, of not really knowing.

Even more difficult for Olga was the uncertainty about John. For three months she had had no word. When the Japanese had taken him away, ill and unconscious, where had they taken him? Had they really taken him to a hospital on the outside, or to another concentration camp? Perhaps he had died. While Olga's bony fingers scrubbed away on the washboard, hot tears dripped off her face into the water. She stopped now and again to give relief to her raw knuckles.

With John gone, only her faith in God carried her through. But how lonely she was without him, and how she missed his calm, steady support! John would never let himself submit to complete discouragement.

The washboard was a good place to scrub away emotions, so she remained there for some time.

As the morning lengthened, more people milled around the camp. Underfed children, pale and thin, strayed listlessly here and there, not caring to play. Olga noticed Mrs. Miller wheel a baby carriage out into a sunny spot, park it, and walk away. This day, like all others, promised nothing but dull and uneventful hours. No matter what kind of irregularities occurred, few seemed to care. Illness, births, deaths—each only a pause before the next dreaded event. While the silence of the uncaring covered the camp like a gloomy pall, Olga's thoughts soaked up her share of lethargy.

Suddenly, out of nowhere it seemed, a piercing shriek shattered the silence. Olga looked up from her washboard to see a woman standing on the outside of the double row of barbed wires, waving her hands. For all her incoherent screaming, she seemed to be giving a message. Olga walked as close to the barbed wire as she dared and listened. What was the woman trying to say? Olga caught the word "war." Whatever she was saying, she kept repeating it, and suddenly it made sense to Olga. She was proclaiming in her native Chinese, "The war is OVER! The war is OVER!"

Olga walked toward a tree and fell to her knees. Strange what war will do to people. Dear God, had that woman lost her mind? Yet the shrieks continued, and brought others close to the barbed wire to listen. Olga felt herself shaking all over. Could the woman be telling the truth? Wanting to grasp at the thin straw, yet fearing the woman's proclamation might be a cruel hoax, she pleaded, "Dear God, is it true? Is it true? Please tell me. Give me some sign."

As she knelt and prayed, wanting desperately to climb over the black wall that imprisoned her mind, the sudden roar of a plane directly overhead brought her to her feet. The plane seemed to be circling the camp.

Was it friend or foe? Where were the guards? Why didn't they open fire? She concluded it must be a Japanese plane. Soon another roared into view, and another, and another. Still no fire. Now the full tone of the camp's bell was heard. Four times it pealed—the signal for all prisoners outside to get into their rooms and stay there. As she hurried to obey, she noticed that the Miller baby was still in its buggy and the mother was nowhere in sight. Olga decided to wheel the baby inside.

Before she could reach him, she saw a tremendous object of some kind, about the size of a piano, hurtling down from the sky in the direction of the baby. Running as fast as her thin legs would allow, she had almost reached the baby when the object landed with a thunderous bang only eighteen inches from the sleeping infant. Sheer horror froze her in her tracks, but only for a few seconds. Concern for the baby shook her loose. Expecting to find the baby screaming with fright, she couldn't believe her eyes when she saw the baby sleeping peacefully. Olga could almost hear the flutter of the baby's guardian angel. At once, then, she took command of the buggy.

But now other objects were falling from the sky, landing here and there in the compound. Clutching the metal bar of the baby's buggy she zigzagged in every direction to escape getting hit. As the boxes and drums hit the ground, the boxes broke open, spilling hundreds of cans of peaches, pears, apricots, fruit cocktail, and juices all over the ground.

Not all the boxes landed inside the camp. Those which landed outside brought hundreds of ragged and starving Chinese on the run. They clawed for the cans, paying no attention to more boxes and barrels falling from the sky. Some cans burst open on impact with the ground, mixing their contents with the dirt. This food, too, the hungry mob pushed and clawed for, mindless of danger from above. Then the feared possibility happened—one of the plummeting boxes crashed into the middle of a group of Chinese. Wild screams and horrible cries blended with the thud of the falling boxes. Several persons were killed.

Olga witnessed the terrible scene. Reaching a tree, she picked up the baby, still sleeping, and huddled with him as close as she could against the trunk and out of the way of falling objects. Feeling dizzy, she prayed that she would not faint on the spot.

More containers fell and burst open. Coats, pants, dresses, sweaters, and shoes flew in every direction. Then, as suddenly as the planes had come, they circled and flew away.

When Olga's head cleared, she realized what had happened. The screaming woman had been right. The war *must* be over. These planes had been American ones, bringing manna from heaven. Now that the shower of boxes had ceased, men, women, and children came running and shouting from every direction. Women screamed and cried. Children wept and whimpered. Even men wept unashamedly, and some uttered oaths of pleasure. All grabbed cans and packages. Some found nails and used them to pound holes in the cans, drinking juice until they almost popped.

Others smashed the cans open by hitting them against hard objects. Using their fingers, they wolfed the contents like famished animals. Manners were forgotten, as all sought to fill their starving stomachs. Packages containing candy and gum were opened and devoured. Even Olga found her Hershey bar.

But, oh, that night, how their stomachs ached! Bodies deprived so long, could not endure the shock, and everyone, without exception, vomited the food he had consumed. One man was heard to say, "It tasted just as good coming up as it did going down."

When all had calmed down, the camp superintendent ordered roll call. Everyone mustered outside with great excitement. Olga could hardly wait to hear what he had to say. Facing the hundreds of happy prisoners, Mr. Drew could not hide his own happiness. "Yes, it's true. The war is *over*. In fact, the guards have already left this camp, and we think the commandant has also gone."

Roars of cheers filled the air. Mr. Drew lifted his hands for silence. "However, we have reason to believe that there may be a few guards lurking in the bushes ready to shoot *anyone* who dares to make a break for it right now. As your superintendent, I must order all of you to remain here until instructions and orders come from the Red Cross."

While overwhelming gratitude and happiness now filled Olga's heart, anxiety to know what had happened to her husband filled her with impatience. Now that the war was over she must go and find him. Well, she told herself, she would wait until tomorrow— but not a moment longer. Guards or no guards, she was going out to look for her husband. But for now, thank God, the war was *over*.

The War Ends | 15

The next morning was Sabbath. The excitement, the noise of the joyous internees spending the night in celebration, and the anticipation of getting out to find John had kept Olga awake most of the night. But she rose bright and early and was hurrying to take a cold shower in the drafty bathhouse when she heard voices yelling from across the barbed wire. "The war is over. The war is over." The Chinese words were music to her ears.

Today she would look for John! Very determinedly she found Mr. Drew and told him her plan. "I'm going out now that the war has ended, to find my husband." A glow, absent from her face for many months, now illuminated her whole being. "And I would like your permission to leave," she finished.

A look of concern came over Mr. Drew. "Mrs. Oss, as much as I would like to, I cannot give you permission to leave until we receive official orders for our release. Surely you can wait another day or so."

"No, Mr. Drew, I cannot wait another day."

"Perhaps you don't realize that danger still lurks around these barbed wires. There may be guards in ambush just waiting for someone to make a move. They would not hesitate to open fire." He frowned.

"But the guards have all left," Olga insisted.

"Yes, they smuggled their *furiskes* (bundles of clothes) and guns and left. And although no one saw him leave, the commandant has also gone." Mr. Drew rose from the chair and walked to the window. "But we have reason to believe that out there in the bushes around the barbed wires Japanese soldiers still wait."

"I must go *now* to find John." Her voice trembled.

"Mrs. Oss, the streets are filled with rioters and looters and killers; and if you insist on leaving, I cannot take the responsibility. You will have to sign out at your own risk."

Desperately Olga assured him, "Oh, I'll be glad to take the responsibility." She could not endure one more moment of delay.

And so, in her thin, wrinkled voile dress, pieces of cardboard in her shoes, and without hose, she walked slowly past the first row of barbed wires, past the next row, and through the big iron gates—the first prisoner to leave the camp on her own two feet. Once she was outside the gate, two young Chinese with bicycles spotted her and came directly to her.

"You are an American from that prison camp, are you not?" asked one.

Olga eyed him with suspicion, "Yes, I am."

The young man smiled kindly. "Here, take my bicycle and use it to take you wherever you are going."

Taken by surprise at the young man's generosity, because in all her years in China no Chinese in the street had ever offered his bicycle, she groped for words. "But—but—young man, I have no money."

"You do not need money. I want to lend you my bicycle, because you are an American and suffered in that prison camp." The words came quickly.

A rush of gratitude came over her. "All right, young man, I want to get to the Seventh-day Adventist Church on Tibet Road at the Y.M.C.A." She moved to mount the bicycle, but stumbled. Her legs were too weak. Seeing her about to fall, the young men reached to give her support.

"Here, let us help you," they offered. Unable to refuse, she allowed the young men to take the handlebars and push her through the streets of Shanghai to the Y.M.C.A. building where the Adventists were having services at 9:30.

"If you will wait here, I'll go in and get some money to pay you," Olga offered. Then seeing their surprise, she added, "I have friends inside the church."

She hurried into the church and came out at once, only to find the young men gone. Tears of humble gratitude filled her eyes as she reflected on the kindness of these anonymous benefactors.

Quietly she entered the large double door and slipped into the last seat at the back of the church. Services had already started, and a group sat on the platform. Because the Chinese are very reverent in their services, she did not want to disturb them now.

All at once one of the men on the platform recognized her. He acted as though he had seen a ghost. Forgetting church he shouted, "Mrs. Oss has come. Mrs. Oss has come!" All those on the platform ran down the aisle to greet her, smiling and crying at the same time. Questions flew from all directions.

"Where is Elder Oss? Why isn't he here? How did you get out?"

"I don't know where my husband is. Have any of you seen him? They took him away, critically ill, from camp, three months ago. And I have heard nothing from him." It was so hard to keep from sobbing now that she was among friends. She did not want to break down in front of these people, because the Chinese are somewhat stoical and do not cry easily over trials and even death. They show little of their emotions.

In the group were Pastor Hsu Hwa, Mrs. Laing of the silver opium box, and many friends whom she had known for years before internment. Among them was the little old lady, whose feet had been frozen off, who dragged herself along the streets on Sabbath morning, never missing a church service.

Pastor Hsu Hwa shook her hand vigorously. "We prayed for you," he said.

Mrs. Laing embraced her warmly. "Oh, Mrs. Oss, I saw John when he was in the hospital the first time. Did he tell you?"

"Yes, John told me how you sneaked into the hospital and brought him money for food. My dear, you saved his life." Olga returned her embrace. Then she asked, "But how did you get past the guards? John said he heard their footsteps and their clatter all the time you were there. He was afraid they would discover you and harm you."

Mrs. Laing smiled. "Mrs. Oss, you and Elder Oss taught me to trust in God. Elder Oss need not have been afraid. God shut the guards' eyes and ears, and they did not hear or see me." Her words came with simple sincerity.

"But how did you know John was in the hospital?"

"Pastor Hsu Hwa told me. I have been reading the Bible, and it says that a man will lay down his life for his friends," said the woman who once had worshiped idols.

Unable to hold back her tears any longer, Olga sobbed, "Oh, thank God for friends like all of you."

"How thin you are!" Mrs. Laing observed.

As Olga watched her friends, something about their attitude told her they did not know that the war was really over. "The war is *over*. It is official," she announced. All rejoiced, forgetting that they had met together for formal church services.

"Will you help me to find John?" she asked Pastor Hsu Hwa.

"Of course," was his quick reply, "but first we will have prayer."

After a season of devout and grateful prayer, they hired pedicabs for Pastor Hsu Hwa and Olga.

"Let's go first to the General Hospital," Olga suggested. Then she added, "That's where they took him the first time, you know."

The streets were filled with throngs of excited people. Havoc seemed to reign on every hand. As the coolies pumped their way over the bumpy pavement, Olga noted widespread evidence of looting. Distraught mobs wandered aimlessly, causing the coolies to veer from side to side.

When they reached the hospital, the first thing Olga noticed was the absence of any guards. "The guards are gone," she burst out.

"Yes, it seems that way, but we must be careful," warned Pastor Hsu Hwa. Cautiously they found their way to the main desk, where a Chinese nurse was on duty. She looked up when she saw them.

Coming to the point, Pastor Hsu Hwa asked, "Do you have a John Oss registered in the prison ward of this hospital?"

Breathlessly Olga waited for the nurse's reply.

The nurse flipped through a box of filed cards. Looking up, she informed them, "Yes, Mr. Oss is on fourth floor." Her eyes went from Pastor Hsu Hwa to Olga's colorless face. "He is very, very ill," she added.

Olga felt her knees buckling. Pastor Hsu Hwa noticed her weakness and reached out to support her. "Come, now, I will help you up the stairs."

"John is alive. Oh, thank God, John is alive," were the only words she could utter. She wondered if she would faint before they reached the fourth floor, but with Pastor Hsu Hwa's firm support she made it, and they soon located the room the nurse had designated.

Pastor Hsu Hwa flung open the door. John lay in bed, too sick to move, too weak to speak. His eyes indicated recognition, but nothing else. Olga bent over her husband and threw her arms around his form, weeping. "Oh, John, John, thank God you are alive!" She repeated the words over and over.

Suddenly Olga straightened. She felt her strength, born of determination, returning. Facing Pastor Hsu Hwa, she cried, "Let's get him out of this hospital. Let's take him to our Adventist clinic."

Pastor Hsu Hwa nodded. The clinic was located across Soo-Chow Creek. During the war people had been fearful to cross creeks, because the Japanese lay in ambush ready to mow down with machine guns any who might try to cross. Now the coast seemed clear. Yet stray bullets still occasionally whined through the air to terrify people.

Pastor Hsu Hwa and Olga left John in the prison ward and made their way out again into the debris-strewn streets and across the creek to the Adventist hospital. To their surprise they found that the institution was still being operated by the Adventists. They were informed that the Japanese had requisitioned two stories for their wounded soldiers. Before the war Dr. Chen, on the Adventist staff, had cured the wife of a Japanese commander. The officer, not forgetting the doctor's good work, had therefore allowed the hospital to remain in the hands of the Adventists.

Conditions now, however, were deplorable. The section operated by the Japanese was badly in need of disinfectants. Dirt lay in corners, and bedbugs crawled over the beds.

Olga and the pastor searched for and found Dr. Chen. When they told him about John, the good Christian doctor wept. "Yes, yes, we'll send an ambulance immediately to get Elder Oss. We'll prepare a room for him."

Olga and Pastor Hsu Hwa returned to the General Hospital, confident now that John would be in good care. Olga kissed her husband tenderly as gentle hands placed him in the ambulance. Then she remembered her promise to Mr. Drew, to return to camp that night.

Pastor Hsu Hwa escorted her and did not leave her until she had passed safely through the gates of the prison camp. Mr. Drew seemed greatly relieved to see her. "You are fortunate, Mrs. Oss, that all fared well with you. Today several of our Britishers decided to leave camp too and lost their lives. They were killed in the streets."

Olga was exhausted, but this day would always be a memorable one. This day God's promise had been fulfilled, "I will never leave thee, nor forsake thee."

Angel of Death Gets Cheated | 16

Olga opened her eyes next morning to find everything in commotion. The iron gates had been opened, albeit unofficially, and a steady flow of people, rickshas, and pedicabs streamed through. Friends brought cakes, sugarcane, cases of canned milk, and many other goodies the prisoners had not seen for months. Men as well as women wept unashamedly and hugged each other. Morale that had sunk to the lowest depths now rose with exhilaration.

As she milled with the throngs, Olga noticed a pedicab pulling up to the gate. Two familiar faces caught her eye immediately. But she could not believe what she saw. She recognized a cherished friend, Mrs. Wong. But the woman with her—who was that? Surely not the friend's mother. She knew that the elderly woman hated foreigners and was openly hostile to missionaries. She had always ignored Olga in a most rude manner.

Nevertheless, in spite of misgivings, Olga was thrilled and waited for them to come closer so she could greet them.

When they spotted her, the old mother snapped into action. Picking up a black urn of solid bronze at her feet, she alighted and walked toward Olga. Her daughter, following close behind, kept saying, "Mother, let me carry the urn. It is too heavy for you."

Ignoring her daughter, the gray-haired lady walked with the heavy urn right up to Olga. Holding it out with both hands, she bowed very low and spoke humbly. "Mrs. Oss, I have come to this camp to give you this urn. It is more than 600 years old. It has been in the Wong family for centuries. Many have burned incense and worshiped at this urn. Now I don't need it anymore. Because you and your husband stayed in concentration camp, I am a baptized member of the Seventh-day Adventist Church. And I will tell you why. My daughter, Catherine, who stands here now, once knew the world—"

As the elderly woman talked on and on telling her story, Olga found herself reliving the scenes that had brought their lives together:

She saw a black ambulance racing over the hard pavement of Rubicon Road, weaving in and out of traffic and blending into the dark night. The lights of Shanghai had streaked past its draped windows in a mad constellation. The driver, too, had seemed mad on spanning in moments the fourteen miles to the neat and quiet buildings of the Shanghai Sanitarium and Hospital.

Inside the ambulance, the black angel of death had waited to hurl a final blow. Catherine Wong, doll-faced daughter of wealth, educated in private schools, heir to many stores in Shanghai, faced the grim lifetaker. Behind the ambulance had raced the vehicle that carried her coffin. And what a dazzling beauty it was—black with gold edges, buffed like pure glass. The inside was frothy with waves of Peking pure red silk. The softly cushioned folds lay in readiness—anxious to caress their captive.

With the wail of its desperate siren piercing the night air, the ambulance had pulled into the driveway of emergency quarters. Quickly the dying woman was wheeled into the very best room the hospital had to offer. Moments heavy with the weight of eternity had slipped by. Later in the operating room, surgeons in white worked quickly and silently, until the gray-haired surgeon broke the silence. "TB, terminal stage," he announced. "Let's close up the hip." No other words came from Dr. Miller as the unsuccessful operation came to a close.

In the days that had followed, Catherine Wong waited. And the coffin waited. When the doctors told her that she would die, a fatal despair seized her. Fully aware that her coffin had followed, she waited, stupefied, frightened, and sad.

One afternoon Dr. Miller's aunt, a Bible instructor, along with a Chinese Bible worker, came to Catherine's room. They opened the door quietly and peeked in. Catherine's eyes were open, simply staring at nothing.

"May I come in?" whispered the missionary lady.

Mrs. Wong's eyes seemed not to care, yet her voice said, "Please come in."

Mrs. Miller had glanced at Mrs. Wong's hospital chart and knew her desperate condition. She took note of the faithful servant who stood beside her bed, never leaving her. The young servant bowed, smiled, seeming happy to see them.

Mrs. Miller reached for Catherine Wong's still white hand. "I am Mrs. Miller," she smiled. "May I show you some pictures?" In her hand she held a long roll of paper.

The tiny voice invited, "Yes, please do."

Unrolling the picture roll, Mrs. Miller had held it up for Mrs. Wong to see. The patient's eyes came to rest on the colored picture of a tall, beautiful, and majestic angel, standing by an empty tomb and saying, "He is not here. He is risen."

Catherine Wong was a Buddhist, worshiping at the shrines of her religion. Daily she had burned incense in the black urn of solid bronze that had been in the family for 600 years. And now, for the first time, she glimpsed another God—the God of Christianity.

"Tell me about the picture," she urged softly.

Not wanting to tire the patient, Mrs. Miller hurriedly turned page after page of the picture roll, relating the plan of redemption and the story of Christ and His love. She did not leave out the promise of resurrection and the gift of immortality that God will give to those who love Him and keep His commandments. The complete plan was unfolded before the woman destined soon to lie in her coffin.

Soft tears filled the sick woman's eyes. They seemed to say, "Oh, if only, if only I could believe all this. If only I could really believe that if I died today, one day I would rise in the bloom of youth and live eternally."

How could she make herself believe all this? What kind eyes Mrs. Miller had. And that little crippled Chinese worker—how sweet her smile.

Catherine Wong could not see beyond the tears.

Mrs. Miller and her crippled associate knelt to pray. While Mrs. Miller lifted her voice with intense supplication, Mrs. Wong's eyes remained open, and through her tears she saw the earnest face of the suppliant offering prayer in her behalf.

"Yet not our will, but Thine be done," ended Mrs. Miller, and rose to her feet. With a smile she moved toward the door.

"Tomorrow?" questioned Mrs. Wong.

"Yes, we will come back tomorrow," promised Mrs. Miller. After the door had closed, for the first time in many hours Catherine Wong forgot her coffin and fell asleep. She slept through the night. Beside her bed, sworn never to leave her, sat her loyal servant.

Early the next morning Dr. Miller came into the room. With deft fingers he prepared to lift the abdominal bandages and to clean and pack the diseased hip.

A look of anger suddenly crossed his face. Turning to the servant he asked, "What have you done? Why did you remove the pins? Don't you know that infection might set in?"

The girl cowered. "No, no. I did not touch it."

The doctor lifted the large bandage. Then he gasped, and his mouth hung loosely. Underneath the bandage lay the piece of gauze that had covered her wound, neatly folded and lying on her abdomen. And the incision—the once ugly incision—unless his eyes were deceiving him, was healed. He fingered the scar. The wound was closed, clean, and healed over.

His voice filled with incredulity, he gasped, "Why, this gauze is folded. The wound is healed!" The shock of it all left him a little faint.

Mrs. Wong was saying, "Doctor, I don't have any more pain. I want to get up and walk."

"No, no, you mustn't do that," said the distraught doctor. Turning to the young servant whom he knew never left the room, he asked, "Did—who—what—did anyone come into this room last night? How can this be?" His eyes demanded an answer.

The girl seemed surprised. "Don't you know what happened last night?"

"No, tell me quickly," urged the doctor.

Shaking with excitement, the girl spoke to her mistress rather than to the doctor. "Do you remember the American lady and the crippled Chinese who came into your room yesterday and showed you pictures?"

"Yes, yes."

"Those *nagatung-si* [angels] were in your room last night. They went to your bed and *ta men moi mo* [put their hands under the cover on your wound]. Oh, I was so scared. Oh, my heart and my liver!" She placed her hands on her chest and abdomen.

Now the astonishment left the doctor's eyes. Reverence and humility shone through instead. "This is a miracle. This is a miracle. God has answered our prayers." Dr. Miller was a praying doctor, and compassion for his patients had often sent him to his knees.

He recognized the hand of the divine Physician when he saw it. The disease that would have claimed the life of Catherine Wong had disappeared. Mrs. Wong was pronounced fully healed and left the hospital. The story quickly spread, especially the part about the Buddhist girl who had watched a miracle take place.

During the days that followed this remarkable sequence of incidents, Olga too had become acquainted with Catherine Wong, and a friendship fabricated by the unbreakable threads of Christianity had developed. Furthermore, through Mrs. Miller's and her united efforts, Catherine Wong had accepted the God who had healed her. She was baptized and became a staunch member of the Seventh-day Adventist Church on Range Road.

Catherine Wong's mother was still talking, "I thought it was our Buddhist god who healed my daughter. But when I stayed with my daughter and her husband, and heard them cry and pray to *your* God to deliver you from the hands of the enemy and keep you alive, somehow, I wanted to give my heart to *your* God. Imagine, my daughter praying for two foreigners!" Now with shaking hands she placed the urn in Olga's hands.

"I want you to have this urn—to remember—to remember— that because you and your husband were missionaries in China, my daughter and I came to know your God."

Through her tears, Olga smiled. She had never calculated the cost of mission service, but at this moment the price of thirty-one months in a concentration camp seemed exceedingly small compared with the happiness that was now hers.

God Is Not Dead 17

Mr. Drew continued to warn the jubilant prisoners that none should leave the camp until official word came from American sources. It was not long before the proper authorization came. And then it also became known that the last orders received by the commandant and the sixteen guards had been to kill every single prisoner in camp if American forces should land in Japan. Oh, how thankful Olga was that God had stayed the destroyer's hand.

Even yet, Japanese snipers lurked around the camp, and internees had to move with caution. When Mr. Drew called Olga to tell her that there was someone at the gate to see her, she felt a little apprehensive. Was it a trick? Were snipers scheming to kill her? She found herself trembling. On the other hand, it might be some word about her husband. She would go.

Pushing her fears aside, she walked to the gate, her eyes searching the area. A small man stood outside the barbed wire. Looking at him closer, Olga recognized a Mr. Ah Mee, a servant at the mission compound.

When the man saw her approaching, he came closer. "Oh, Mrs. Oss, you must come at once. The Japanese are looting the sanitarium. They are stealing doors and windows and even cutting down the trees." His voice was filled with excitement.

"Ah Mee, it is so good to see you," Olga greeted, "but how distressing the news you bring! However, I simply cannot come now. But I will give you a note to take to Pastor Hsu Hwa. He will take care of things." Olga left and returned at once with the note. The man took the message to Pastor Hsu Hwa, who in turn went to the police. They arrived in time to save the sanitarium from being torn apart brick by brick. Again God's hand had intervened.

On Monday, Olga received official permission to leave the camp to see her husband, as now the area seemed fairly safe. Olga found him at the clinic where the ambulance had taken him. Every doctor in the hospital had examined him. Along with serious anemia, he was suffering from an undiagnosed disease which the doctors agreed was causing him to lapse into spells of unconsciousness, and which would, if unchecked, surely take his life.

Now Olga became desperate. John couldn't die now! Now that freedom was theirs. She remembered that two of the newest prisoners in camp were doctors. They were German Jews, reputed to be among the world's most brilliant medical men. When Dr. Chen heard about them, he decided to call them to examine John. They both agreed, after extensive examination, that John was suffering from a brain tumor. "Only immediate surgery will save his life," said one.

Olga was shocked. Now John could not eat. He had to be fed intravenously. As she watched her husband, almost lifeless and still in a world of unconsciousness, she prayed, "Dear God, there must be some other way for John besides surgery." She was very reluctant to give her consent for the operation. John was too weak, she feared.

Dr. Chen advised, "Olga, unless you give your consent, John will die. There is no doubt in my mind now that he has a brain tumor." Still she could not bring herself to agree to surgery. In her heart she hoped for another solution.

At least there was one more thing they could do—they could pray. A group of faithful Chinese Adventist friends decided to take a room across the hall from John and pray with open Bible, twenty-four hours a day. By now Olga had moved into a hospital room, and she joined them.

Several days passed, with John sinking lower and lower. On Sabbath morning Dr. Chen went to Olga. "Please come to church with me this morning," he invited kindly.

Feeling tired and dejected, Olga replied, "I'll stay with John. I would rather."

Dr. Chen persisted. "Don't worry about John. I will leave two nurses with him."

His persistence touched her. Wearily she agreed to go. The church was filled with Chinese believers. Olga was the only white woman. Dr. Chen rose to make the announcement. "My dear brethren," he began, "our beloved Elder Oss is dying. Only God can save him now. Today will be a special day of fasting and prayer for Elder Oss." With a choked voice he continued, "First, we must make our own hearts right with God, then we will have special prayer."

It seemed to Olga that angels were present at that meeting, as she knelt with friends whose faith spanned oceans of difficulty. Pastor Hsu Hwa led in prayer, and the presence of the Holy Spirit came upon them. There was not a dry eye in the group.

At the hospital, two nurses hovered beside the unconscious form of John Oss. Neither spoke a word as they waited, fearing the end. The moments passed—one by one. Suddenly a slight flutter of John's eyelids brought the nurses to attention. Slowly he opened his eyes. First he looked at the ceiling, then around the room, and finally at the nurses by his side. For the first time in five days John was conscious. Then he spoke—slowly but clearly. "Nurse, will you bring me a piece of paper?"

One nurse jumped to find the paper, while the other remained by his bed. "I would like a pencil too," he requested. The startled nurse returned quickly with both items.

Lifting his head slightly, John Oss scrawled these words: "Olga, God has healed me." Then his head fell back on the pillow.

It was still morning when Dr. Chen and Olga returned to the hospital. As they hurried into John's room, they could not believe their eyes. They found John fully conscious, eyes open wide and bright, and speaking the first words he had uttered in weeks. "Where have you been, dear, and where am I?" he asked feebly.

Olga fell on the bed and pressed a gentle kiss on his lips. "We've been to church—praying for you." She wiped her eyes and smiled. The fullness of God's Spirit still welled up in her heart.

"Olga," John said softly, "I've been healed."

Olga thought her heart would burst. Dr. Chen wept tears of joy. "Call the nurse," John requested.

The nurse came with the note he had scribbled and handed the paper to Olga. Her hands trembled as she read, "Olga, God has healed me." Recognizing it had been penned earlier while they were engaged in prayer at the church, she understood. Was anything too hard for God?

Dr. Chen examined John at once, checking factors significant to a physician. "He appears to be normal." Turning to Olga he said, "Please let me take the note back to church right now to show the people before they go home."

No one doubted that God had healed John. But anxious to hear what the German doctors would say, Dr. Chen called in the two men for another consultation.

Now John's mind was clear as a bell. When the two doctors arrived, eager to examine him, John could not know that they had been there before and had only a short time before declared his death sentence. He asked, "Who are these men, Olga? Why do you not introduce them to me?" Carefully the doctors examined him, making all kinds of necessary tests. Their report was, "We find no symptoms of brain tumor anymore, no symptoms of any disease!" Looking puzzled but very pleased, they added, "This man is healed."

A short time later John and Olga were homeward bound on the beautiful new hospital ship the U.S.S. *Sanctuary,* principally used to carry wounded and sick servicemen out of the war zones. The luxury liner, with its beautiful wide corridors and spacious rooms, placidly plowed the waters of the vast Pacific.

At the Presidio in San Francisco, John was again examined by doctors, and no sign of brain tumor could they find. He was sent to the White Memorial Hospital in Los Angeles for further tests, and the result was the same. John had been healed by prayer.

The God who had been their refuge and strength in a faraway and strange land, the God who had watched over them through days of imprisonment, discouragement, and hunger, the God who had provided manna from heaven, was the living God, the God who had performed the miracle of healing. Their God was not dead.

Back in the States again, John and Olga were not content with what they called a "dull life." They requested another term overseas and landed back in Shanghai on Thanksgiving Day, 1947. For three more exciting and rewarding years they continued to serve the people who had come to mean more to them than their own kinfolk—friends who never failed them, not even during that worst ordeal of their lives, internment days behind barbed wire.